Thank you so much
Sandra
for your help!

I wish you
great success
in Toronto!

Success In Toronto: A Guide for New Immigrants

Hirantha Nandasena

AuthorHouse™
1663 Liberty Drive
Bloomington, IN 47403
www.authorhouse.com
Phone: 1-800-839-8640

© 2011 Hirantha Nandasena. All rights reserved.

No part of this book may be reproduced, stored in a retrieval system, or transmitted by any means without the written permission of the author.

First published by AuthorHouse 4/4/2011

ISBN: 978-1-4567-5876-9 (e)
ISBN: 978-1-4567-5877-6 (sc)

Library of Congress Control Number: 2011905190

Printed in the United States of America

Any people depicted in stock imagery provided by Thinkstock are models, and such images are being used for illustrative purposes only. Certain stock imagery © Thinkstock.

This book is printed on acid-free paper.

Because of the dynamic nature of the Internet, any web addresses or links contained in this book may have changed since publication and may no longer be valid. The views expressed in this work are solely those of the author and do not necessarily reflect the views of the publisher, and the publisher hereby disclaims any responsibility for them.

Legal disclaimer

This book is a work of non-fiction. The author and the publisher make no explicit guarantees as to the accuracy of the information contained in this book and in some cases, names of people and places have been altered to protect their privacy.

Before initiating any of the strategies outlined, seek the advice of a competent professional to help you. This book is intended as a general guide only and further research is needed and assistance must be sought from a qualified expert before any action is taken by the reader.

This book might contain errors, omissions, or mistakes of either a typographical nature or within the content itself. The reader must not rely on the accuracy of any of the information given, but should seek proper verification.

The author (Hirantha Nandasena) and publisher shall have neither liability nor responsibility to any person or other legal entity with respect to any sort of loss or damage or perceived damage caused, or alleged to have been caused by the information provided in this book. By reading this book, you fully accept these conditions.

Acknowledgments

I would like to thank my dad, Attanayake Nandasena; mom Lalani Nandasena; my three brothers, Prasanna, Aruna and Sanjeewa; relatives; friends; and teachers for all the help given throughout these years and most importantly for being there in times good and bad. I would also like to thank everyone including Magdalena Gjesvold and Fiona Wilson, who encouraged me to finish this book as soon as possible. Finally, I would like to thank everyone who helped me publish this book.

Here's a poem I wrote few years ago. I never studied poetry so please forgive me if you think it's the worst poem you've read in your life.

I'm in Love With an Angel

I'm in love with an angel …

Her eyes are blue, her hair is golden

So soft has been, every word she's spoken

Her smile is sparkling, so soft she's walking

Feels like I'm in heaven

'cause, I'm in love with an angel …

As I look into her eyes, full of emotion

Feels like I'm staring at a beautiful blue ocean

My heart is pounding, my words are trembling

I don't know what to do, I don't know what to say

Then I realize, all I need to say

is, I love you

Foreword

Success in Toronto: A Guide for New Immigrants, by Hirantha Nandasena, signifies a landmark for us in Toronto, since it represents the first book of its kind made available to new immigrants who struggle for a foothold after having arrived with glowing hopes. The work is clear and comprehensive with the critical areas well explained and prioritised.

The presentation begins with general information and then proceeds to the specifics for easy understanding. "Being Positive" and "The Good Things of Canada" are dealt with at the outset in order to encourage the new immigrant not to lose heart and then lose way. The author then embarks on topics like the things to be done in the first two weeks, handling the winter, quick and easy ways to improve English, how to save, etc., which are all vital considerations for any new immigrant. The critical and mandatory items to be attended to as early as possible, such as applying for a Social Insurance Number and a health card, are structured and fitted in appropriately to facilitate smooth reading. The specifics, such as finding a place to live based on one's needs and circumstances and locating the closest public library for free use of computers, are dealt with in due course.

I have no hesitation in recommending Success in Toronto to all the institutions engaged in servicing new immigrants in such subject areas as settling in, finding employment, seeking guidance on the services available, etc.

Finally, I wish to express my deep appreciation and to thank the author for the valuable service rendered in compiling this useful material for ready use.

Daya Hettiarachchi

Introduction

My friend, I wrote this book to help the thousands of immigrants who migrate to Toronto to settle down here and achieve great success. By Toronto, I mean the Greater Toronto Area, which includes cities like Toronto, North York, Scarborough, Missisauga, Brampton, Etobicoke, Markham, and more. I felt the need for a book like this because I haven't seen or heard of a book on this topic. Please see the value of this book to a new immigrant and recommend it to them. Think about all of the time, money, etc., they could save by reading this book. I also believe that this book will be able to give them some direction to follow to achieve success. Having said that, I must also state that this book is valuable not only for new immigrants but for anyone in Toronto who wants to learn how to succeed here. It will show you how to live a great life here in Toronto and how to be proud to be Canadian.

Please refer this book to all of your friends, relatives, and co-workers etc. so more will benefit from it. It will also help me be financially independent and then I can spend more time on more versions of this book and spend more time on helping people in any way I can. Actually, since the age of sixteen, my goal in life has been to retire (be financially independent) at thirty and then help people by doing charity work. I have seen through my own eyes how people suffer without food, shelter, and education etc. and I am determined to help them and make a difference.

It gives me much pleasure that I have published this book, especially because, when I migrated to Canada, I did not have any relatives, friends, a proper job, a car, or many other things, and the weather (especially in winter) was pretty harsh for me. Add to that homesickness and I think you agree that such a situation can be pretty depressing.

I tried to limit the number of pages without affecting the quality because I know from experience that, especially when you are new to Canada, time is very limited. I also tried to use simple English without fancy words because, for many of you, English is probably your second language and I don't want language to be a barrier. I've included one joke in each chapter to make it a bit more interesting.

I sincerely hope that this book will help you to achieve great success in this new place you now call home. Please send any feedback to me at info@successintoronto.com. This will help me improve this book and publish a second version (perhaps an extended version or part two) soon. Enjoy!

Contents

Legal disclaimer	v
Acknowledgments	vii
Foreword	xi
Introduction	xiii
Chapter 1—The Twelve Main Principles	1

    (1) Save a minimum of $50,000 in five years
    (2) Network with others
    (3) Focus on solutions to problems and take action
    (4) Have a plan and monitor your progress
    (5) Have a budget and stick to it
    (6) Get advice from the correct people
    (7) Firmly believe you will succeed
    (8) Always be positive
    (9) Change what you can
    (10) Change your circumstances to improve chances of success
    (11) Be at least a little religious/spiritual
    (12) Experience what you couldn't have

Chapter 2—Good Things about Canada	11

    Multicultural society
    After some time, it feels like home here
    Weather is not so bad

Peaceful country
  Good education
  Good healthcare system
  Good for current and/or future children and grandchildren
  Close to USA (Florida, Hawaii, etc.)
  Franchises like McDonalds, KFC, Pizza Hut etc. are so affordable
  Seasonal changes

Chapter 3—Having Fun for Little Money — 17
  Be Happy
  (1) Bluffers Park
  (2) Ashbridge's Bay Park
  (3) Sibbald Point Provincial Park
  (4) Wasaga beach
  (5) Niagara Falls
  (6) Marineland
  (7) High Park Toronto
  (8) Search for comedies, TV shows, films, sports, etc. on YouTube
  (9) Find songs, recipes, movies, TV shows, etc., on cultural sites
  (10) Coupon sites like Redflagdeals.com
  (11) JDRF Walk
  (12) Grayline Tours of Toronto
  13) Skype instructions

Chapter 4 – What to Do in the First Two Weeks — 41
  Open a bank account
  Get private health insurance
  Buy clothes
  Find the closest grocery stores

Find a place to live
Apply for the Health Card and SIN (Social Insurance Number)
Start building your contacts
Learn about the TTC (Toronto Transit Commission)
Go to the library for computer access
Apply for the Canada Child Tax Benefit (CCTB)
Get a land phone, cell phone, Internet, and TV
Register kids in a school
Start your job search
Go to downtown Toronto and one of the three popular malls
Buy a computer

Chapter 5—Finding a Place to Live   51
Tips on renting an apartment
Tips on buying a new house
Tips on buying a used house
Tips on buying a condo

Chapter 6—Finding a Great Job   61
How to get a great job
Get your credentials assessed
Embrace Diversity

Chapter 7—Travelling (Day Trips and Long Distance)   69

Chapter 8—Buying a Car   75
Get a driver's license
Change your address for driving license within six days of a move
Have to change parking ticket address separately

    Great twenty-four hour garages (for vehicle repairs)
    Get the CAA Membership
    Buying a new car
    Buying a used car

Chapter 9—Handling the Winter   83
    Layering

Chapter 10—Saving   87
    The three e's (efficient, effective and economical)
    Rain Checks
    Good products
    Good Stores
    Twenty-four hour restaurants
    Creating a credit history
    How to get rid of your change
    Be careful when lending money
    Emergency fund
    Make your own coffee
    A cheap way to go to the airport
    How to get out of a cell phone contract

Chapter 11—Investing   99
    Registered Retirement Savings Plan
    Registered Education Savings Plan

Chapter 12—Cooking in Less than Twenty Minutes 103

Chapter 13—A Quick and Easy Way to Improve English   107

Chapter 14—Assistance   115
    Settlement assistance (overall)
    Legal aid
    Employment Insurance (EI)

Social Assistance

Chapter 15–Important Contact Phone
Numbers and Websites   123
   Emergency contact number
   Telephone directory

Chapter 16—Conclusion   131

Chapter 1—The Twelve Main Principles

Here are the twelve main principles:

(1) Save a minimum of $50,000 in five years

As explained in Chapter 10, "Saving", your main goal is to save $800 per month with low risk, which means you'll have $50,967.7 in five years (at 3 percent interest per year). Time flies, and if you don't follow this plan, after five years you will wish you did. Please note that you will probably have to reduce this financial target if you plan to sacrifice time for studying, volunteering, etc.

(2) Network with others

Most of you probably didn't realize it but, before migrating to Canada, we had a network of people and contacts that we approached when we needed to get something done. Many of these people were automatically available to us because of our family, friends, where we lived, religious institutions, and so forth, and our networks had grown over the years. This is invaluable for success. Now that we have moved away from the old network, what we have to do is develop such a network here, too. This is not that hard. Just create new friends who work in the industry you want to work in. Befriend people who share the same ideals. Befriend people who enjoy and are willing to help others. After some time, you will find that you have a network of people and contacts like you had in the country you migrated from. Then, you will find it much easier to find a good job; you can perhaps borrow something you need to get something done, you can get some good advice, etc. Life becomes so much easier when you have such a network. You will have to search for some of these contacts, but some will come to you automatically over the years.

(3) Focus on solutions to problems and take action

If you are facing problems, instead of worrying about them, write them down in a list and try to come up with solutions for them. Then take action. Try to be creative, get advice from others, observe what others have done to overcome similar problems, etc. Worrying just drains your energy and your problems won't go away. Just to illustrate, list one problem at the top of one blank paper and stare at it and worry about it for five minutes. Has anything changed? Did the problem go away? Of course not. Now, spend another five minutes trying to think creatively of solutions and writing them down on the piece of paper. If you cannot come up with solutions, spend more time until you come up with some solutions. As you can see, the second approach is much better. Once you have found a good solution, take action to implement it. Only then will you see the results. Finding creative and effective solutions to your problems will definitely help you succeed in life.

(4) Have a plan and monitor your progress

Decide on a list of things you want to get done in the next six to twelve months to improve your chances of getting a great job. For example, you might decide to get a driver's license, get your credentials assessed from WES (World Education Services), complete a three-month co-op program, develop a relationship with five people who work in your field, get credits for your qualifications from an educational institution, and enroll in a course related to your field. It's not hard to get all of this done within six to twelve months. For example, I told a new immigrant who lives in my building to do this two months ago and now he has a driver's license, credits from CMA (Chartered Management Accountants), more than five friends who are accountants, and he has a good chance to sign up for a co-op program for accountants that starts in two more months. According to our six to twelve month plan, all he has left to do is to get his credentials assessed by WES, enroll in a CMA course, and sign up for the co-op program. Both he and his wife are working part time so they can cover their expenses. If you have a list of items like this and get them done, it will be a great achievement. If not, after your first year in Canada, you may find that you haven't really got much done because you did not have a clear focus. Track your progress at the end of every month to ensure you get things done. Also, have a five-year plan like this and monitor your progress. Effectively getting things done is very important for success.

(5) Have a budget and stick to it

It is important to have a budget for your monthly expenses and to ensure that you do not exceed it. This gives you great control over your expenses. There are many good books and articles on budgeting so please find a good one and read it. Budgeting is very important not only in Toronto but anywhere in the world.

(6) Get advice from the correct people

I included this as a principle because, when I was new, I was getting advice sometimes even without asking, from different people. I ended up being confused and not knowing whose advice to follow. So, when selecting one or more persons to get advice from, look for these qualities:

- Has been successful in the area you are getting advice about.
- Is willing to give advice to others and share their knowledge.
- Has been in Canada for some time, especially if you are getting general advice about cultural values, handling the winter, etc. More than ten years would be good.
- Has a positive attitude.

(7) Firmly believe you will succeed

What is success? Many think it is all about making a lot of money. But, success is not just about money but also about being happy, being healthy, having loving relationships, having a job you like, spiritual development, career advancement, having time to enjoy life, and enjoying a good home environment.

When you firmly believe you will achieve something, your chances of success are much higher. Many celebrities, such as athletes, actors, and highly successful businessmen, consider this the key to success. When you have a firm belief that you will achieve something, your subconscious mind will guide you to achieve it. When you have a firm belief, you will automatically be dedicated to achieving it. The universe, too, will pick up your desires and will help you achieve them.

Just one great example is Barack Obama becoming the first black president of USA. Do you think that fifty or a hundred years ago (even ten years ago) people would have thought this would be possible? But, with great determination to change the circumstances, great leaders inspired African Americans to press for change and believe that they could change the future.

Another example is India and China becoming dominant players in the world scene. Even twenty years ago, this was not the case, but with the desire to improve their circumstances they have emerged as the new dominant players of the world.

Do you think that the players in any of the examples above would have achieved these outstanding results if there was no strong desire and belief to succeed?

(8) Always be positive

I do understand that it's not always easy to be positive,

especially when we keep having bad experiences. But remembering these will help you to be positive:

- Somewhere along the way, you will come across opportunities. If you are not positive, you might not be tempted to grab these opportunities and improve your circumstances.

- When you are positive, you send out a positive signal to the universe and, in return, you will get positive results.

- When you are positive, people around you (employers, family, and friends) want to be around you and they are willing to help you because it appears that you will positively use whatever help they offer to improve your circumstances.

(9) Change what you can

Change what you can to improve your circumstances. One good exercise is to list the problems you have on a piece of paper. In an exercise book, write these down using one page for each problem. Then, on each of these pages, write down what you can do to resolve the problem or at least minimize the effects of the problem. Here, you can also get advice from someone experienced and successful. Try to be creative in finding solutions.

After writing down possible solutions, you'll be amazed at how many of your problems can be resolved or effects minimized by taking action. Don't you think doing an exercise like this and then taking action to resolve a problem is much better than keep on worrying about your problems ? The key is to "Take action". If you just keep worrying and do nothing, nothing will change. It's when you start taking action that you see things improving.

One thing you can improve is your home. Whether it is just a room, an apartment, or a house, you can spend one day to get rid of the clutter and make it neat, organized, and pleasant. If you don't know how to, please get the help of a friend who is good at it. Once you do this, you can see that by taking action, you made a positive change in your life. Having a neat and pleasant place is good because you know that no matter what you go through during the day, you can always be assured that your home is a pleasant place to be.

(10) Change your circumstances to improve chances of success

If you want to achieve something, do the following to improve your chances of success. You may even call this improving your chances of being lucky.

- Start talking and dealing with the people who might be helpful.
- Acquire relevant resources.
- Change the way you think and act.
- Spend more time and/or money on this.

As an example, if you want a job in your industry, try doing the following:

- Start talking and dealing with the people who might be helpful.

E.g., Invite friends who already have jobs in your industry to dinners, barbecues, etc., and ask them how you can get a job in their industry.

- Acquire relevant resources.

  E.g., Buy or borrow a very good suit to wear for interviews.

- Change the way you think and act.

  E.g., If your aim is to be a project manager, you have to think, talk, and act like a project manager. You will need to have good negotiating skills, be able to manage people, be able to communicate well, etc.

- Spend more time and/or money on this.

  E.g., If a few friends who work in the industry recommended a very good certificate program that employers look for, enroll in that course and spend enough time to obtain the certificate.

> *Friend: hey, what are you doing with a pen and paper?*
> *Me: I am writing a letter to my brother*
> *Friend: I thought you didn't know how to write.*
> *Me: Doesn't matter, my brother can't read.*

(11) Be at least a little religious/spiritual

It's totally up to you, but I would suggest that you learn to be at least a bit religious/spiritual. I say this because religion can teach us some good principles in life such as helping others, not causing harm to others, and so forth. When you do good things, good things happen to you. Just as an example, imagine that you are someone who always tries to be honest; you never steal even if a friend tempts you to. After few years, a close friend of yours who works at a bank branch as a teller is asked to refer someone for a job. Won't he give preference to you over others? He will feel comfortable that the chances of you stealing any money from the bank is very low. Even if you don't have a friend working for a bank, your friends may refer you to any cashier jobs that they come across.

Since I have an open mind, I've been trying to study different religions. I do not want to offend anyone in any way but, as I understand, the main religions do mention that if you do something good, you will get something good back in return. Similarly, if you do something bad, you will get something bad in return. In Buddhism and Hinduism, this is known as karma. In Christianity, the Bible mentions that "whatsoever a man soweth, that shall he reap." I apologize that I don't know the wordings on this topic in other religions.

(12) Experience what you couldn't have

We migrated to Canada to improve our lives and experience a different country that has a high standard of living. So, try to experience what you could not have in the country you migrated from. I have explained more about this in Chapter 2, "Good things about Canada." This way you can be satisfied that you did experience these different things that you may have seen in movies or read about in books or magazines but perhaps wouldn't have been able to experience in the country you migrated from. After all, life is about experiencing different things.

Chapter 2—Good Things about Canada

Here I have tried to describe briefly some good things about Canada. This is to help you be positive. Especially when you are new to Canada, you might feel negative because your standard of living might have gone down. For example, you may discover that you can't find a job that suits your qualifications, the winter weather is cold, and you have no proper facilities in the place you live.

So, try to look at the positives like the ones listed below. Remember, being positive is essential to achieve success.

Multicultural society

Canada is a multicultural country with people from many countries and many languages spoken. Especially in Toronto, you can see how diverse the people are. Diversity is good because we can meet people from different countries and learn about their cultures, way of living, food, and so forth. This enriches our lives. Don't you enjoy at least one kind of food other than traditional Canadian, such as Chinese, Indian, Italian, Greek, or Mediterranean?

For me, diversity is even more interesting because, like many people, I always wanted to travel and experience different parts of the world. Now, even though I cannot actually see the different parts of the world without travelling, for free I can talk to/visit the homes of people from different countries and learn first-hand from them about their countries and cultures. Such conversations will also help me select the places I would like to visit and have a better time when I get there.

Another benefit to living in Canada is that many countries are probably closer to Canada than the country you migrated from. Here, we can travel at a cheaper rate to Florida, Miami, California, and other states in the United States of America; to the Caribbean or to South American countries like Brazil and Argentina; and even European countries like Italy, England, Switzerland, France, and Greece. It's also fun to explore cities in Canada like Vancouver, Halifax, and, of course, let's not forget Toronto.

After some time, it feels like home here

After maybe two to five years, it feels like home here. When you are new, you might feel homesick because, in your country, you knew how to get to places, how to get a job, and you had friends, family, relatives, and neighbors for support. As the old saying goes, "Time heals everything." After a few years, you'll have more friends, and some of your old friends and family might have migrated here. They will make life easier and more interesting and will provide you with a support base. After a few years, you will have gained some experience and contacts, which will mean you probably have a job in your field of expertise. At least, you will have a job better than the one you had when you first arrived in Canada.

Weather is not so bad

Okay, before you disagree with this statement, please read on. I came to Canada from Sri Lanka. When I was new to Canada, I was worried about the cold weather. I was used to temperatures above 20°C throughout the year in Sri Lanka, and I thought, "Oh my God, I'll get such temperatures only two or three months of the year and that means that 75 percent of the year, I will struggle with the weather." But now, I realize that the weather is bad mainly in the winter, which lasts only two to four months. This can be okay as long as I have a car at least for the winter. By the way, if you want a car just for few months of the year, I know that at least State Farm Insurance does not tie you into a one-year contract. After a few years, my body has adjusted to the fall and spring weather conditions and now I actually like having four seasons in the year. In fact, I actually think having warm weather throughout the year is a little boring because it is so predictable. I enjoy the clear and crisp air in the cooler months. If you wear proper clothing, the weather is not so bad.

Peaceful country

Quite a few of us have come here from countries where crime, killings, war, corruption, low human rights, low women's rights, and other woes are prevalent. Sometimes we don't realize how peaceful Canada is. Your rights are protected, and if that's not the case, you can always stand up for yourself and be heard. You have rights! Having a peaceful environment is important.

Good education

Canada has a world-class education system. Not only you but your current and/or future children and grandchildren can benefit from this.

Good healthcare system

Another thing that is world class in Canada is its healthcare system. Some of the medical equipment at our disposal here for free is not available in many countries, and even if it is, you probably would have to pay exorbitant amounts to use it at a private hospital.

Good for current and/or future children and grandchildren

Your current and/or future children and grandchildren stand to benefit from the world-class education and healthcare systems and everything else Canada has to offer. They probably will not face the hardships of the first generations here because this will be their home country and, just like the countries where we were brought up in feel like home, they will feel comfortable here. Since they will be educated here and will have enough contacts from university, different jobs, social activities, and friends, finding good jobs related to their studies and being able to live happy and fulfilling lives should not be hard. The motivating factor for you to live here is knowing that your efforts will result in a better future for your children. Many people who descended from immigrants don't feel like moving to their parents' country if they were brought up in Canada. They say, "This is my country." Some of you might not like this because you want your children and grandchildren to remember their heritage, so I must add that most or all of these same people still practice their parents' cultures and do visit their parents' countries.

Close to USA (Florida, Hawaii, etc.)

Canada is close to the USA, sharing a long border, and it is fairly cheap to travel to famous places like Florida, Hawaii, California, and New York. You've most likely seen such places on TV or in movies or heard many good things about them, so it would be a good life experience to visit one or more of these places.

> *Me: Teacher, would you punish me for something I never did?*
> *Teacher: Of course not. I would never do something like that.*
> *Me: Good, because I never did my homework.*

Franchises like McDonalds, KFC, Pizza Hut etc. are so affordable

Franchises like McDonald's, KFC, Pizza Hut, etc., are so affordable here so visit one or more of these places once in a while. I say this because the price of one meal at one of these places is a small fraction of your monthly income;

this is probably not the case if you migrated here from a developing country. You've most likely seen such places on TV, in movies, or read about them, so it would be a good life experience to visit one or more of these places.

Seasonal changes

After two to five years, you will get used to the weather and will start to like the changes of season. Having a vehicle will really help you with this because your body will be shielded to a great extent from extreme weather conditions. It's kind of nice that the weather is not the always the same, because that can get boring. Also, each season has its own fun activities:

Summer—Get outside to enjoy activities like visiting beaches, Niagara Falls, Marineland, camping, etc.

Fall—Enjoy watching the color of the leaves change and start watching the Raptors (Toronto's basketball team) and the Maple Leafs (Toronto's ice hockey team).

Winter—Enjoy the holiday season, read books, watch the Raptors and the Maple Leafs as they battle for a playoff spot.

Spring—Watch the flowers blossom and the trees grow leaves, watch the basketball and hockey playoffs (hopefully with the Raptors and the Maple Leafs).

Chapter 3—Having Fun for Little Money

Here are just few things you could do to have fun with little or no money:

- Hang out with friends
- Dine at different restaurants
- Watch sports with friends
- Go to night clubs
- Go to a beach
- Skate in front of City Hall
- Visit AGO (Art Gallery of Ontario)
- Watch movies at home or at a theater
- Go to a mall

- Visit Chinatown (Spadina Road @ Dundas Street West)
- Visit Kensington Market (Spadina Road @ Dundas Street West)
- Visit Greek Town (Broadview Avenue @ Danforth Avenue)
- Visit Little India (Gerrard Street @ Ashdale Avenue)
- Visit Korea Town (Bathurst Street @ Bloor Street West)
- Visit Little Italy (College Street @ Bathurst Street)
- Visit Portugal Village (Dundas Street West @ Bathurst Street)
- Do some charity work
- Visit Toronto Islands
- Visit the harbor front
- Visit Casa Loma
- Visit the Ontario Science Centre
- Visit the Toronto Zoo
- Go downtown and just walk around
- Join some group that shares your interests

Buying the CityPASS is a good deal because you get to visit the CN Tower, Casa Loma, the Ontario Science Centre, the Royal Ontario Museum and the Toronto Zoo for almost half the price compared to individual entry fees.

For more information, please visit:

http://www.citypass.com/toronto

Be Happy

We work hard so we can be happy, so what's the point if we keep working hard without being happy? One thing that I do is watch around ten minutes of comedy on YouTube every day. This helps lift my spirits and like the saying goes, laughter is the best medicine. Another way to stay happy is to make your life in Toronto an adventure. Below, I have provided brief descriptions, maps, and directions for just a few places to make it easy for you to find them. The objective is for you to find out about other places (ask friends, read tourism guides, search in Google, etc.) that might interest you and visit them.

Hirantha Nandasena

(1) Bluffers Park

This beach just south of Kingston Road on Brimley Road is a nice and relaxing place because it has a parklike setting surrounded by trees. There are also few grills that you can use for a barbecue. You might want to take water, food, drinks, folding chairs (available at Wal-Mart, Canadian Tire, etc., for around $15 each), or sports items like a football, a volleyball, badminton rackets with shuttlecocks, etc. There are washrooms. Here is the map and directions:

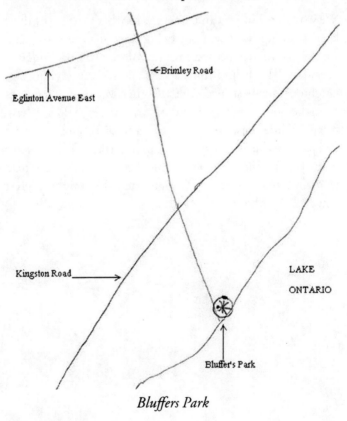

Bluffers Park

By bus:

From the Kennedy subway, take bus #12B and tell the bus driver to drop you as close as possible to Bluffers Park (at the intersection of Kingston Road at Brimley Road). Go south on Brimley Road until you see the park.

By vehicle:

If you are coming from the north, just keep going south on Brimley Road past Kingston Road until you see the park.

If you are coming from the east, take St. Clair Avenue East and make a left at Brimley Road, then keep going until you see the park after Kingston Road.

If you are coming from the west, take St. Clair Avenue East or Eglinton Avenue East and make a right at Brimley Road, then keep going until you see the park after Kingston Road.

(2) Ashbridge's Bay Park

This is another beach similar to Bluffers Park. Here is the map and directions:

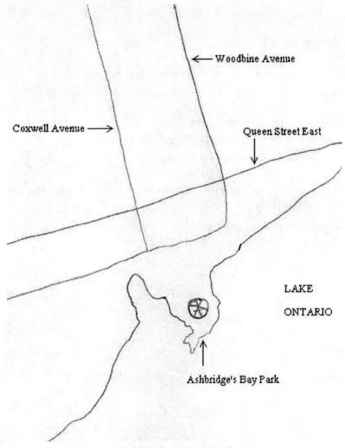

Ashbridge's Bay Park

By bus:

From the Coxwell subway, take bus #22 and tell the bus driver to drop you as close as possible to Ashbridge's Bay Park (just after Queen Street East). Continue walking south, in the opposite direction from which you came, on Coxwell Avenue until you see the park.

By vehicle:

If you are coming from the north, just keep going south on Coxwell Avenue past Queen Street East until you see the park.

If you are coming from the east, take Queen Street East, make a left at Coxwell Avenue, and keep going until you see the park.

If you are coming from the west, take Queen Street East, make a right at Coxwell Avenue, and keep going until you see the park.

Hirantha Nandasena

(3) Sibbald Point Provincial Park

This, again, is a beach similar to Bluffers Park, but the main difference is that it is around one and a half hours driving distance away from downtown Toronto so you will feel that you got a break from the busy lifestyle of the city. It is in the countryside and there are tons of trees so you will feel very close to nature. Here are the map and directions:

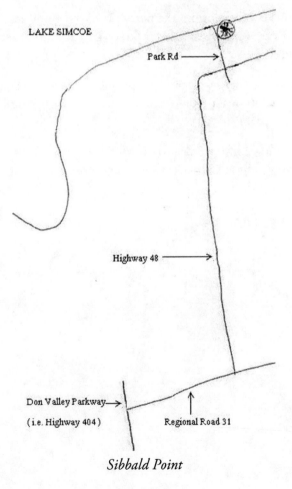

Sibbald Point

By vehicle:

- Take the highway 404 and exit eastbound on Regional Road 31.

- Make a left (northbound) at highway 48.

- Make a left at Park Road and continue until you see the beach.

Please take a map and/or a GPS with you because it is a remote area and there probably will not be many people around to help you if you get lost.

(4) Wasaga beach

This is similar to Simcoe beach but is perhaps more popular. Here is the map:

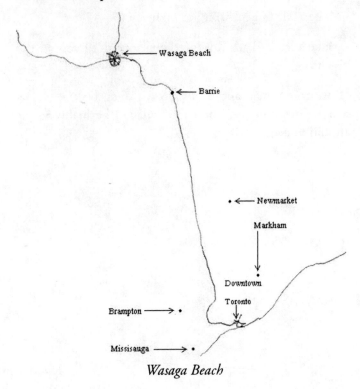

Wasaga Beach

Since the directions are a bit complicated and it's a good time for you to start using Google Maps for directions, please get the directions by doing the following:

- Do a search for the postal code L9Z 1A1 in Google.

- Click the map that appears.

- Click "Directions" in the left middle area.

- Enter your address in the box where the cursor is (labeled "A").

- Click "Get Directions."

(5) Niagara Falls

This is one of the most popular tourist destinations in the world because of its beauty. There you also get a break from the busy lifestyle of the city.

Other than the falls, some area attractions are the floral clock (a clock shape on the ground made of flowering plants), wineries, Niagara On The Lake, the casino, various fun stores in front of the falls, etc. Although it takes a full day to enjoy Niagara Falls in a relaxed way, if you do have some time, you can cross the border to Buffalo, New York, in the United States (passport or visa required) for some shopping.

Try the helicopter sightseeing tour if you can afford it. At the time of writing, the price for an adult is $118 and $73 for a child. The flight lasts nine minutes and covers twenty-seven kilometers over Niagara Falls. For more info, go to www.niagarahelicopters.com or call 1-800-281-8034.

Another attraction is the Jet Boat Tour. At the time of writing, the price of an adult ticket is $59 and $49 for youth. The tour lasts sixty minutes. For more info, go to www.whirlpooljet.com or call 1-888-438-4444.

Here is the map:

Success In Toronto: A Guide for New Immigrants

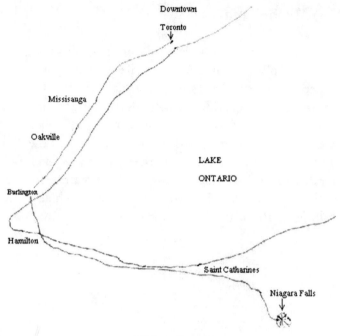

Marine Land

Since the directions are a bit complicated, please get the directions by doing the following:

- Do a search for the postal code L2G 7X5 in Google.

- Click the map that appears.

- Click "Directions" in the left middle area.

- Enter your address in the box where the cursor is (labeled "A").

- Click "Get Directions."

(6) Marineland

Marineland, just one mile (1.5 km) from Niagara Falls, is a great place to visit. As the name suggests, you get to experience marine life as they have dolphin shows, whale shows, and an aquarium as well as other attractions. They also have a roller coaster, other rides, and an area where you are surrounded by a lot of deer. You can also feed the deer with food sold at the counter in the deer area. When I took food to them, I was surrounded by like about twenty deer and it was a wonderful experience. You need a whole day to fully enjoy this place. Here is the map:

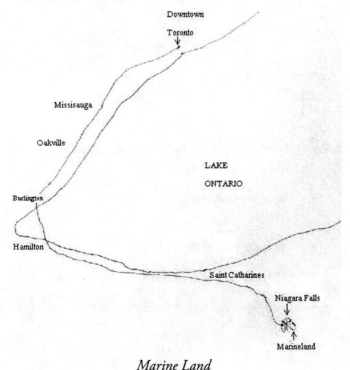

Marine Land

Again, the directions are a bit complicated so, please get the directions by doing the following:

- Do a search for the postal code L2E 6X8 in Google.
- Click the map that appears.
- Click "Directions" in the left middle area.
- Enter your address in the box where the cursor is (labeled "A").
- Click "Get Directions."

(7) High Park Toronto

High Park is Toronto's largest public park, featuring many hiking trails, sports facilities, great scenery, a beautiful lakefront, TTC access, a dog park, a zoo, playgrounds for children, a great restaurant, greenhouses, picnic areas, and more. I went there this year (2010) and had a great time. The great thing is that it is close to downtown Toronto (at Keele Subway) but, because it is huge (three hundred and ninety-nine acres), once you go to the middle of the park, you won't feel that you are close to downtown.

www.highparktoronto.com has more details about the park. The address is:

High Park, 1873 Bloor Street West, Toronto, ON M6R 2Z3, Canada.

For more information about High Park, call the City of Toronto Customer Service Centre at (416) 338-0338.

(8) Search for comedies, TV shows, films, sports, etc. on YouTube

There is lots of free but great stuff on YouTube. Just type "funny animals," "comedy," or the name of your favorite comedian, you'll find some really funny stuff. You can also search for some of your favorite TV shows by searching by name. The good thing, too, is that you can find some old shows that are not aired anymore, or not aired in Canada. Some films are also available and again, just search by the title of the movie. Some sports are also available. For example, I search for cricket (the game) highlights or special moments in its history (e.g., best catch, best innings, legends of the game, etc.). I've noticed that some sports events are viewable live and sometimes for free. For example, I watched the semifinals and finals of a major cricket tournament (IPL—Indian Premier League Twenty 20) for free.

> *Me: Bro, I've heard that frogs never go to psychiatrists. Is that true?*
> *Frog: Yup, we just eat what bugs us.*

Hirantha Nandasena

(9) Find songs, recipes, movies, TV shows, etc., on cultural sites

You can find the latest news, songs, recipes, movies, TV shows, and much more on some cultural sites. Please ask your friends who share the same cultural values (e.g., from your country of origin, etc.) which sites are good. You may also ask a cultural association, place of worship, etc. For example, I go to www.infolanka.com everyday to get the latest news from Sri Lanka. They also have links to the websites of popular Sri Lankan newspapers, and links to songs, recipes, etc. Have fun for free! It's also important to do the same for the Canadian culture and be proud to be Canadian.

(10) Coupon sites like Redflagdeals.com

Try this and other websites for good discounts on various things (groceries, movies, clothes, etc.). For example, you might get a two-for-one movie coupon, which is a great deal if you like going to the movies. You can also add yourself to the e-mail mailing lists of your favorite stores like Gap, Levi's, etc. You can also view online the flyers of your favorite stores by visiting their websites. Also try www.entertainment.com for more coupons.

(11) JDRF Walk

The JDRF (Juvenile Diabetes Research Foundation) Walk is held in the summer. It's a great way to enjoy a summer day with friends, family, and others while contributing to a great cause. Your happiness will be multiplied because you'll feel great supporting a worthwhile cause and enjoying a nice and relaxed summer day while walking your way to healthiness. For more information, please visit www.JDRF.ca.

(12) Grayline Tours of Toronto

Please visit www.grayline.ca or call 1-800-594-3310 and consider some of the tours they have. Here are some examples:

- North/south loop
- East/west loop
- Greater Toronto Tour and harbor cruise
- Toronto Hippo Tours. This is a ninety-minute tour of Toronto on both land and water on the amphibious bus "The Hippo."

13) Skype instructions

Skype is a computer application that you can download for free and use to make free calls and free video calls to any computer in the world. You can also make calls to land and cell phones, but for these a fee may apply. Imagine being able to make a video call to your loved ones in another country for free. If the download speed of the other party's Internet connection is too slow to view live videos properly, just ask them to go for just an hour to a communication center that has Skype. Even if the communication center doesn't have it, you can download it as shown below with their permission. Just try it with one person and both of you will love it. I use it to make live video calls to my family in Sri Lanka and to my best friend who lives in Halifax. Because I really believe you will enjoy Skype, here are the instructions on how to download and use it:

- Go to www.Skype.ca.
- Click "Join" at the top.
- Fill in your information, click "Continue," and follow the steps.

Once you have downloaded the Skype program, if it is not already open, double click the "Skype" icon on your desktop to sign in if you are not already signed in.

How to make a call to a land phone or a cellphone

Please note that you could be charged for this call. For more information, please visit the Skype website at www.skype.ca

- Click the "Call Phones" button at the bottom left corner.

- Enter the number either by clicking the buttons on the dial pad or clicking the area where it says "Enter number."

- Click "Save" on the dial pad if you would like to save the number.

- Click "Call" on the dial pad to start the call.

How to add a new person to your contacts list

- Click "Contacts" in the menu at the top.

- Click "New Contact."

- Search for the person by entering the person's Skype name, full name, or e-mail address.

- Click "Find" and complete the steps to finish adding the person.

How to make a call to anyone anywhere in the world free of charge

This sounds like a great deal but the other person must also have Skype installed on their computer.

- If you have not already done so, add the person to your contacts list as shown above.

- Click the person's name on your contacts list that appears on the left side.

- Click the "Call" button that appears in the top middle.

How to make a video call to anyone anywhere in the world for free of charge

Hirantha Nandasena

This is the best feature of Skype because you can see the person live while talking to them. Please note that if the Internet and computer speed of yours or the other party's is very slow, you might not get a good quality video call.

- If you have not already done so, add the person to your contacts list as shown above.

- Click the person's name on your contacts list that appears on the left side.

- Click the "Video Call" button that appears in the top middle.

Chapter 4 – What to Do in the First Two Weeks

Here are some things to do in the first two weeks in Toronto.

Open a bank account

This is one of the first few things you should do as soon as you arrive in Canada. Go to the nearest bank with two pieces of identification (e.g., your landing papers and passport) and open an account. After a month or two, see if you have been charged additional "per transaction" fees for performing more transactions than allowed by your bank account plan. If so, talk to the bank and see what plan is best for you and change to it. Some banks have special account plans for new immigrants, including ones with no monthly service charge. The big six banks in Canada are Royal Bank, TD Canada Trust, Bank of Nova Scotia, Bank of Montreal, CIBC (Canadian Imperial Bank of Commerce), and National bank.

Hirantha Nandasena

Get private health insurance

Ontario Health Insurance Plan (OHIP) requires a three-month waiting period before coverage begins. In the meantime, if you have to go to the doctor or hospital, you'll have to pay for it and it could be very expensive (even thousands of dollars). So, if you did not arrange for private health insurance for you and your family before coming to Canada, do it as soon as you arrive. Contact a private insurance company directly or call the Canadian Life and Health Insurance Association Inc. at 1-800-268-8099 to find one. Examples are Broker Advantage at 1-877-294-1810 (www.brokeradvantageinc.com) or Manulife at 1-888-626-8543 (www.manulife.ca) or TIC Insurance at 1-800-379-9628 (www.travelinsurance.ca). They might require you to sign up before or within five days of arrival in Canada. If you are not in Canada yet, try asking your embassy to recommend an insurance company.

Buy clothes

Especially if you arrive in Canada during the fall or winter, one of the first things you should do is buy some clothes that will keep you warm and comfortable. Ask someone or check online to see where the closest Wal-Mart is and pay a visit.

Find the closest grocery stores

Ask your neighbors where they shop. They've probably been in the area for some time and know the best places to shop. If not, check online for a No Frills (www.shopnofrills.ca) or Metro (www.metro.ca) store.

Find a place to live

Please read Chapter 5 to learn how to find a good place to live. Please be careful because, if you sign a lease for an apartment, you'll be stuck there for a minimum of one year.

Apply for the Health Card and SIN (Social Insurance Number)

To apply for the Health Card,

1. Go in person to your nearest Health Card Services—OHIP office. You can find a location by going to www.ontario.ca/en/services_for_residents/STEL02_186323

2. Complete a registration for Ontario Health Coverage form (Form 0265-82) and they will take your picture for the card.

3. Provide the necessary original documents. For the documents needed, call 1-800-268-1154. Usually you'll need to take your passport, Permanent Resident Card, and something with your name and address, like a bank account statement, but please call before you go there to ensure you do not waste your time travelling.

As mentioned earlier, there is a three-month waiting period for the Ontario Health Insurance Plan (OHIP) coverage. You'll need the health card to access services offered by a doctor or a hospital. The website for the ministry of health is www.health.gov.on.ca.

Apply for the SIN (Social Insurance Number) at a Service Canada location. The SIN number is very important and is needed to work in Canada, to have access to government programs and benefits, for income tax purposes, to apply for credit, etc. To apply for it, you'll need your Permanent Resident Card issued by Citizenship and Immigration Canada. This is the only acceptable document if your claim was processed in Canada.

If you don't have the Permanent Resident Card, you'll need the Confirmation of Permanent Residence AND a visa counterfoil affixed to a foreign passport or a travel document.

Here are the contact details of Service Canada for SIN purposes:

Tel: 1-800-206-7218

www.servicecanada.gc.ca/eng/sc/sin/index.shtml

Start building your contacts

Contacts are so important to be successful in Canada. At the beginning, you will need at least a few contacts just to find out where to shop, how to travel, etc. If you don't know anyone, start by contacting your place of worship. Usually, they help out new immigrants or at least point them in the right direction.

Learn about the TTC (Toronto Transit Commission)

Please read Chapter 7, "Travelling," to figure out how to travel. One of the first things you should do is get a free TTC map from a subway station and mark your home location on it. Also, always keep your address and nearest intersection in your wallet. This way, even if you get lost, you can always show it to a TTC driver and get directions to get back home.

Go to the library for computer access

At the library, you can use their computers to browse the Internet so, it's a good place to go until you buy a computer and get your own Internet connection.

Apply for the Canada Child Tax Benefit (CCTB)

You should apply for the CCTB as soon as possible. It is a non-taxable amount paid monthly to help eligible families with the cost of raising children under eighteen years of age. Also included with the CCTB is the National Child Benefit Supplement (NCBS), a monthly benefit for low-income families with children.

You will need to complete three forms and you will need your SIN number. Go to the Canada Revenue Agency (CRA) website at www.cra.gc.ca. In the search box, search for the three forms, RC66SCH, RC66, and CTB9.

Here are the full names of the forms but you don't need to type the full name when searching for them:

RC66SCH Status In Canada/Statement Of Income

RC66 Canada Child Benefits Application

CTB9 Canada Child Tax Benefit Statement

Once completed, if you are a in Toronto, mail them to:

Sudbury Tax Centre
1050 Notre Dame Avenue
Sudbury ON
P3A 5C1

As procedures could change, please visit the CRA website to confirm this procedure before following it.

Here are the contact details:

1-800-387-1193

www.cra-arc.gc.ca/bnfts/cctb/menu-eng.html

The general CRA website is www.cra-arc.gc.ca

Get a land phone, cell phone, Internet, and TV

First, look at how much you can afford per month and decide if you need all four of your options: land phone, cell phone, Internet, and TV. Especially until you get a job, you might want to minimize spending on these services. For example, instead of getting an Internet connection and buying a computer, you could manage by using the computers at the library and HRSDC (Human Resources and Skills Development Canada) centers. If you decide to get an Internet connection and buy a computer, perhaps you don't need cable and a TV and instead could watch videos, past episodes of TV programs, comedies, etc., on You Tube. If you live alone, it might be better to get a cell phone with lots of daytime minutes and no land phone. For example, Fido currently has a $40 per month plan where you get 2,000 anytime minutes. If you do get a land phone, instead of paying around $8 per month for voice mail, you could buy an answering machine and let it record your voice mails for free. If you live with your family, you could get a land phone and a pay as you go cell phone instead of a regular cell phone where you have to pay a monthly fee. By getting a pay as you go phone, you will save the monthly fee and will still be able to contact your family. If you are outside and need to make a longer call to your family at home, you could use a phone at work or a pay phone. Having said that, there are cell phone companies now that offer fairly affordable monthly plans (not pay as you go), so please shop around. Just be very careful if you sign up for a two or three year contract because you will have to pay a high fine (maybe even $200 or more) to get out of the contract early.

Go to a mall like Yorkdale, Eaton Centre, or Scarborough Town Centre and compare the prices and features the stores offer for a land phone, cell phone, Internet, and TV. Many service providers offer three months free Internet if you sign up with them. It's better to go with someone who has been in Canada for few years so that you will not be tricked into buying something you don't need or get locked into a contract. If no one is willing to come with you, go to the stores, get the details of what you plan to sign up for, and show it to a friend before signing up for anything.

Register kids in a school

Ask your neighbors which school in the area is good. I say this because some schools may have a lower crime rate, better teachers, etc. Then, contact either the Public School Board at (416) 397-3000 or the Catholic School Board at (416) 222-8282 to see if the school is within your school boundary and what documents you'll need to register your children. They will also arrange for a learning assessment for your kids. If it's within your school boundary, take your kids and the documents to the school and enroll them. If it's not within your school boundary, ask which one is and go there. If you don't want to call the school boards, try going to the school directly to enroll your children.

Start your job search

Read Chapter 6, "Finding a job," and start your job search. Please remember that the majority of the jobs in Canada are not advertised, so contacts and referrals are very important to get a job.

Go to downtown Toronto and one of the three popular malls

I recommend this so that you will get some taste of the good side of Canada. For example, if you went to a remote area straight from the airport, you might think that's what you can expect from Canada. If that area is not that good, you might be disappointed. Please go to the intersection of Yonge & Dundas in downtown Toronto and visit the Eaton Centre (www.torontoeatoncentre.com) there. Just walk on the streets, have a coffee, take some pictures, etc. You may also visit the Yorkdale Mall (www.yorkdale.com) and/or the mall at the Scarborough Town Centre (www.scarboroughtowncentre.com). Once you can afford it (you've gotten a job and saved some money, for example), try to go somewhere out of the city like Niagara Falls or Wasaga Beach to see what the country is like outside of Toronto.

Buy a computer

If you are buying a new computer, compare prices and features at Best Buy, Future Shop, and Wal-Mart. Do not listen to the salesperson and buy unnecessary accessories. You can buy them later once you get a job.

If you are buying a used computer, please be careful. Ask your friends if they have bought a good used computer and if so, from where. Your friends or contacts at your place of worship may even have a free computer for you. For example, I asked a friend today if she had one for an immigrant family who live in my apartment building, having arrived in Canada just ten days ago. She said she didn't, but would ask around. She is a very busy person, but in an hour and forty-five minutes, she called me to tell me that her boss had one.

I once bought a good used computer from Techdirect at 259 College Street West (College Street and Spadina Avenue), but since I used their service only once, I am not sure if all of the used computers they sell are good. Their phone number is (416) 916-8324 and their website is www.techdirectcanada.ca.

Chapter 5—Finding a Place to Live

In this chapter I will cover:

- Tips on renting an apartment
- Tips on buying a new house
- Tips on buying a used house
- Tips on buying a condo

The two points below are important if you plan to rent:

(1) The law requires the landlord to maintain the standard temperature of a room or apartment at 21°C. This is the standard for Ontario and applies to any time of the year. If the temperature is below 21°C in the winter, I would suggest asking your landlord to make it at least 21°C since it is the standard. If they do not agree, mention that you will have to inform the Ontario Ministry of Municipal Affairs and Housing. Then, they will most likely agree to make it 21°C. If not, just call the ministry at (416) 585-7041 and ask them

to call the landlord or send someone to meet them. The ministry website is www.mah.gov.on.ca.

(2) Did you know that you are entitled to interest on the rent deposit you make when you start renting?

A landlord must pay the tenant interest on the rent deposit every twelve months. The interest rate is the same as the rent increase guideline that is in effect when the interest payment is due. The guideline is set each year by the Ministry of Municipal Affairs and Housing. There are more details you need to know, so please visit the Landlord and Tenant Board website at www.ltb.gov.on.ca. For example, if the rent increases, the landlord may update the rent deposit by deducting the required amount from the interest that is owed to the tenant.

Tips on renting an apartment

I have lived in different apartments and houses, and over the years have learned how to select an apartment or room for rent. The best thing to do is ask a good friend who lives or lived recently in a good apartment and select an apartment in the same building. I say this because, no matter how much you check, there are quite a number of things that can be hidden. For example, if it gets noisy in the evenings, the landlord might try to cover it up by asking you to come to view the apartment only in daytime. If there are roaches in an apartment building, you might not find out until you have lived there for few days or weeks. I can give you numerous examples, but will give just one more: The superintendent could be extra nice to you before signing the lease but when you actually live there, he might take days just to fix something wrong in your apartment, have a bad attitude, or worse. The person you ask should be honest and willing to help others. If you really have to move to an apartment where none of your friends have lived, at least talk to a few of the residents and ask about some of the things listed below.

A lease is a contract, and if you are not careful, you could be stuck for a year with an apartment that you don't like. That said, remember that you have rights and can always contact the Ontario Ministry of Municipal Affairs and Housing for assistance.

Before signing a lease or an application consider the following:

Ask a friend who lives there or used to live there recently or few residents :

- Are problems like plumbing, repairs, etc., fixed in a reasonable amount of time?
- Overall, is the management good and friendly?
- Are there pests like roaches or mice?
- Is it noisy?
- Is the crime rate high?
- Overall, is it a good place to live?

Check:

- Can you afford the rent and any special fees?
- Are there fire exits and functioning smoke detectors?

- Are there any other costs like water, heating, or parking in addition to the rent?

- Do all of the appliances work and how old are they?

- Is the apartment big enough to keep all of your belongings?

- How close is it to your work place? I moved twice to apartments within ten minutes walking distance to work to make life simple and save time and money spent on travelling.

- What is the overall condition of the building and apartment?

- Is there a balcony if you like one?

- Is there an exhaust fan in the kitchen?

- Are pets allowed?

- Is there parking and is it underground?

- Is there public transport to suit your shift of work if you don't drive?

Try to stay away from:

- An apartment on the first floor because it might be easier for thieves to break in and might be noisier with people and vehicles passing by;

- An apartment near an elevator or garbage chute;

- Perhaps not an apartment above the fifth floor

just in case the elevators don't always work. Also remember that if there is a fire alarm, you are not allowed to use the elevators and they might even be out of service. On the other hand, the view from the higher floors most likely is better.

I would prefer a place within walking distance to work or a subway station. Waiting for a bus in a bus stand in the winter could be pretty cold compared to waiting in a subway station or just walking to work.

> *Kid: Yeah! Now I know how to count. One, two, three.*
> *Mom: Very good. Go on ...*
> *Kid: Hmmm, you mean there's more?*

Tips on buying a new house

Below are just the headings for the top ten tips mentioned in the Tarion website and is reproduced here with their permission. The link to the site is http://www.tarion.com/HOME/New+Home+Buyers/Top+Ten+Tips+for+New+Home+Buyers/. I did not include the details of these top ten tips because information changes often. As described on their website, Tarion is "a private corporation that was established in 1976 to protect the rights of new home buyers and regulate new home builders." It continued, "As the regulator of Ontario's new home building industry, Tarion registers new home builders and vendors, enrolls new homes for warranty coverage, investigates illegal building practices, resolves warranty disputes between builders/vendors and homeowners, and promotes high standards of construction among Ontario's new home builders. Tarion also works with the building industry to help educate new home buyers about their warranty rights, and about how to protect and maintain their warranty." For more information, go to www.tarion.ca.

1. Choose the type of home that meets your lifestyle.

2. Determine what you can afford.

3. Research your builder.

4. View our Online Education Seminars

5. Talk with a real estate lawyer.

6. Read our Homeowner Information Package.

7. Prepare for your Pre-Delivery Inspection (PDI).

8. Complete and submit any required Statutory Warranty Forms on time.

9. Maintain your home through the seasons.

10. Enjoy all your new home has to offer!

You've done a lot of research, decision making, and waiting by the time you reach this point. Now it's time to enjoy your new home!

Tips on buying a used house

- Don't buy in a rush. If you hurry, you might have to buy a house that's not ideal for you or that is priced too high.

- Get a pre-approved mortgage. This way, you know the maximum price of the house you can afford.

- Choose a good real estate agent. Ask for referrals from friends who have bought a house recently.

- Choose a good real estate lawyer.

- Location, location, location. If you ask any real estate agent the most important thing to look for when buying a house, this is the answer you will get. Try to find a house that:

    * has a good school nearby

    * is near transportation facilities (subway, buses, etc.)

    * has a hospital nearby

    * has grocery and other stores nearby

    * is close to work

    * has a low crime rate

    * is in an area where selling prices have increased over the years

    * is not near an airport.

- The house preferably should:

    * have a good kitchen and washrooms

    * have a big master bedroom

* have no problems with the roof

* not have been listed for too long.

- Do your own research on www.mls.ca and don't just rely on the real estate agent.

- Check the prices at which similar houses in the area were sold.

- Ask neighbors if it's a good area to buy a house.

- Check to see if the property taxes are affordable.

- Always negotiate the price and try to pay less than the asking price.

- Don't tell anyone how much you are willing to pay for a house. The real estate agent might try to sell it for a higher price because his/her commission is a percentage of the selling price.

- Get a home inspection done before buying.

- Get the house appraised before buying.

- Have extra money for closing costs, lawyers' fees, moving costs, land transfer tax, etc.

Tips on buying a condo

In addition to the tips above, here are some extra tips that apply to condos:

- Check the availability and quality of common facilities such as gym, swimming pool, sauna, etc.

- In general, condos smaller than six hundred square feet are more difficult to re-sell.

- Should have a nice view.

- Make sure your unit is not beside or across from the elevator or garbage chute.

- Do you have a designated parking space?

- Is there a locker to store items not needed daily?

- Is there visitor parking?

- Are the appliances good quality?

- Does the building look good and seem well-maintained?

- Are the monthly maintenance fees affordable?

- Ask some of the residents if it's a good place to live.

- If it has stainless-steel appliances and hardwood floors, the unit will have a higher re-sale value.

- Are most of the residents owners (versus tenants)?

- Does sound travel through neighbors' walls?

Chapter 6—Finding a Great Job

How to get a great job

The main thing is to get into a company that you like and where you think there might be an opportunity for you to land your dream job one day. At the beginning, you might have to do a job you don't like much, but, once you get into a company, it is so much easier to try to get a transfer to a job you love. Many companies also provide in-house or external training and courses to help increase your chances of getting that dream job.

If you are finding it hard to get into a company that you like, at least try to get a job that will help you eventually get your dream job in the company you like. For example, if you would like to work at a bank one day but cannot find a bank job, at least try to get a cashier job at a grocery store and try to complete the Canadian Securities Course. Then, you can show that you are trustworthy, have experience handling cash and customer service, and have a Canadian banking qualification.

As mentioned in Chapter 1 as a main principle, decide on a list of things you want to get done in the next six to twelve months to improve your chances of getting a great job. For example, you might decide to get a driver's license, get your credentials assessed from WES (World Education Services), complete a co-op program, develop a relationship with five people who work in your field, get credits for your qualifications from an educational institution, and enroll in a course related to your field. If you have a list of items like this and get them done, it will be a great achievement. If not, after six to twelve months you might find that you haven't really done much because you did not have a clear focus.

You can also try the normal way of applying for jobs found in advertisements. If you are not responding to a job ad but just trying to find a job in a specific company, I think that at least in some industries (e.g., security, hotels, etc.) it is so much better to apply in person rather than online. Do some research about the organization and learn what they do, why you would like to work for them, etc. Employers really like it if you show that you are really interested in the company and have already put in some effort. Just take a few résumés, dress up well, go to several places you like, and ask for the Human Resources department. Since you are dressed up, try to go to few places that are close to each other in one day. Smile during the interview and it is very important to send a thank-you letter to the hiring manager after an interview. Try to do it within twenty-four hours.

A great percentage of jobs in Canada are not advertised and are filled through referrals. I remember reading somewhere that only 20 percent of jobs are advertised. So, referral is a great way to get a job. Try friends, family, relatives, associations, YMCA, places of worship, and any other groups you know of and you will be amazed at how many jobs are available in this hidden job market. Networking with people is the key to getting a job. In addition to the possibility of a referral, they might also give you great advice. The best advice is from the people who are already doing a job in your field. Friend, I cannot stress how important networking is for your job search. So, if you were to ask me the main point I hope you will learn from this entire chapter, my answer would be, "Networking is very important to getting a great job."

Try HRSDC (Human Resources and Skills Development Canada) centers for job ads, free training on interviews, formatting résumés, use of computers, etc. They also have great workshops that will help increase your chances of getting a job you like.

Get your credentials assessed

To increase your chances of getting a job in your field or to continue your studies, it's important to get your credentials (diplomas, degrees, certificates, etc.) assessed. It's important because it will give your prospective employers or academic institutes a better sense of the value of your credentials. Service Canada Centres provide information, in person or over the phone, related to the assessment and recognition of foreign credentials.

For more information, you may also contact the Foreign Credentials Referral Office at:

www.credentials.gc.ca or
1-888-854-1805.

Another great way to find a job is to go to a job agency. They list lots of jobs and even if you don't get your dream job, the experience you gain from the initial jobs through them will benefit you immensely in your efforts to get that job later. Try asking professionals in your industry which job agencies are best for your industry. For example, I know that Manpower, Kelly Services, and similar firms are good for bank jobs and Accountemps and Robert Half are good for accounting jobs. Once you get a contact person at a job agency, keep in touch with him/her regularly until you get a job. It's better if you get that contact as a referral from a friend.

> *Bird 1: You are an hour late. What happened?*
> *Bird 2: Sorry, man, it is such a nice day so I decided to walk.*

Another great way to find a job in your industry is to do a co-op program. This is a course where you get classroom training and a paid or unpaid job placement for few months. It's great because you get the training and experience all in just program. George Brown University is a great place that has many co-op programs.

Two popular job search sites are www.workopolis.com and www.monster.ca. Please register with them, create a profile, upload your résumé, and apply for jobs there. Employers and job agencies search on these websites for potential candidates for jobs.

What some new immigrant couples do when they are new here is alternate between themselves the effort involved in trying to get a job in their industry. This is because it might not be feasible for both of them to try at the same time. So, while one of them is working full-time and probably doing a part-time job too, the other will put in a great effort to get a job in his/her industry by searching, training, finding referrals, etc. This way, they will be able to focus and have enough time to land a good job. Once he/she gets a good job, it would be the other person's chance.

Your chances of getting a good job in your field will be greatly enhanced if you get a Canadian professional qualification or at least a relevant certificate or diploma. For example, if a new immigrant with an accounting background obtains the CGA (Certified General Accountants) qualification, he/she could probably double his/her annual income.

A good way to increase your income is to have a part-time business. There are also many tax benefits of having a part-time business because the government promotes entrepreneurship. Please speak to your tax advisor for the tax benefits. It's very important to start the business small with low risk and, if things are going great, you can expand later. At the beginning of any business, it takes some time to learn about the industry, human resource management, how to process payroll, government regulations, marketing, gathering information about competitors, etc. Also, if you start small and the business is a failure, you won't lose a lot of money and perhaps could try running some other type of business instead. Try to attend a franchise show like the Business Franchise and Investment Expo to see many franchises that are available. For example, in 2010, it was held the weekend of May 1 at the CNE (Canadian National Exhibition). Purchasing a franchise has advantages and disadvantages. For example, they have quite a number of rules in order to maintain a high standard, but, on the other hand, they might have a proven system that, if followed properly, could bring you great success.

Below are the contact details of HRSDC (Human Resources and Skills Development Canada). They provide information on services provided for job search, service centre locations, etc.

1-800-622-6232
TTY: 1-800-926-9105
www.hrsdc.gc.ca

Once you join an organization, if you think that your rights have been violated, please contact your employee's union. If you don't have a union, contact the Ontario Ministry of Labour. They provide information on employment laws, your rights as an employee, health and safety at work, etc., and below are their contact details.

Website: www.labour.gov.on.ca
Employment Standards Inquiries:
(termination pay, unpaid wages, public holiday pay)
1-800-531-5551
TTY: 1-866-567-8893

Occupational Health and Safety Inquiries:
1-800-268-8013

Report Possible Unsafe Work Practices
1-877-202-0008

Other Inquiries:
1-866-932-7229

Don't be disappointed by setbacks in your job search. It's not that you are not good enough for a job in your field, it's just that you might not be doing your job search properly or that, sometimes, it just takes some time. Once you find the correct way to land your dream job, with some patience, there will be no stopping you. Not everyone can come to Canada. You were selected because you have great skills and qualifications. Do you think that Thomas Edison was successful in inventing something after just one, two or ten experiments? No; he performed thousands of different experiments before finding one right way to do it. That's why they say that, if there is a will, there is a way.

Please go to the intersection of King Street and Bay Street or Yonge Street and Bloor Street at 4:30 p.m. and observe the crowd for thirty minutes. You'll see for yourself that people from various nationalities and backgrounds are trying to go home after working in the offices there. This will give you some confidence, because you can see for yourself that no matter what your nationality or background is, you too can get a good job and prosper.

If you would like to learn more about finding a great job, please read *How to Find a Job in Canada: Common Problems and Effective Solutions,* by Efim Cheinis and Dale Sproule, published by the Oxford University Press.

Embrace Diversity

I humbly request that you embrace diversity and enjoy it rather that use it for prejudice. Try to learn about interesting aspects of different cultures and taste their delicious dishes. If your employer has a diversity council, please join, and if it doesn't have one, encourage your boss to start one. I was a member of such a council and had great experiences while learning more about diversity.

Diversity is based not only on race but also on gender, age, ethnicity, ability, sexual orientation, job status, and knowledge.

Below are some wonderful links that will help you in your job search and settling in Canada. If the links don't work, search the name in Google.

Career Edge:
http://overview.careeredge.ca/index.asp?FirstTime=True&context=0&FromContext=&language=1

Costi:
www.costi.org/whoweare/whoweare.php

Skills for Change:
www.skillsforchange.org/

JVS Toronto:
www.jvstoronto.org/index.php?page=about-jvs

Municipal Internship Program:
www.mah.gov.on.ca/Page16.aspx

Ontario Internship Program:
www.internship.gov.on.ca/mbs/sdb/intern.nsf/LkpWebContent/ePublishedHOME

CanadianCareers.com Internships:
www.canadiancareers.com/internships.html

Employment Ontario:
www.edu.gov.on.ca/eng/tcu/etlanding.html

Good luck with your job search!

Chapter 7—Travelling (Day Trips and Long Distance)

The public transport system (buses, streetcars, underground trains, etc.) of Toronto is known as the TTC (Toronto Transit Commission). Please obtain a TTC map for free from the TTC collectors booth (where you pay the fare) of any subway station. It shows the bus routes with the bus numbers, subway routes with the subway station names, etc. One of the first things you should do is to mark your home location on it. Always keep your address and nearest intersection in your wallet. This way, even if you get lost, you can always show it to a TTC driver and get directions to get back home.

Fares change often so please check the TTC website for up-to-date prices. Here are the fares at the time of writing (November, 2010):

Adult	Senior	Child	Description
$3.00	$2.00	$0.75	1 TTC token is valid for one continuous journey of any distance on regular-fare routes. If you don't have a token, you can pay this amount in cash directly to the TTC collector \ bus driver
5 for $12.50 10 for $25.00	5 for $8.25 10 for $16.50	10 for $5.50	Tokens (bulk discounted)
$121.00	$99.00	Not Applicable	Monthly metropass which can be used to travel anywhere on the TTC during the month indicated on the pass
$111.00	$89.00	Not Applicable	Metropass discount plan
$36.00	$28.00	Not Applicable	Weekly pass which can be used to travel anywhere on the TTC during the week indicated on the pass (Monday to Sunday)
$10.00	$10.00	$10.00	Day pass which can be used to travel anywhere on the TTC on the day indicated on the pass
$52.00	$52.00	$52.00	GTA Weekly pass which can be used to travel anywhere on the TTC, Missisauga, Brampton and York region transit routes during the week indicated on the pass (Monday to Sunday)

TTC Fares

Post-secondary students can buy a metro pass for $99.00 at the time of writing.

Please obtain a transfer where you pay your fare and it can be used to transfer to the next available bus or streetcar where the two routes intersect or serve the same stops. In some cases, two routes operate near each other but do not serve the same intersection and do not have any stops in common. In these cases, where specifically identified, customers can use paper transfers to transfer between routes at the walking transfer locations. For a list of the walking transfer locations, please visit the TTC website at www.TTC.ca and search for "TTC Walking Transfers."

The first time I went to downtown Toronto from Scarborough, I was on my own but with written instructions from a friend. If you are new to Toronto, the easiest way to get to a downtown Toronto location is to take a bus to the subway (underground train) system, take a train to the downtown subway station closest to the place you want to go, and then take a bus, or streetcar, if necessary, or just walk to the location.

The maps published by MapArt are sold at many places including gas stations and are useful because they show many, if not all, roads. The folding map sold for $4.95 and the street guide (looks like a book) sold for $19.95 are good. The folding map is cheap but could be inconvenient if you are driving, because when you unfold it, it is quite large and you need to stretch your arms quite a bit. But the good thing is, once you unfold it, it becomes one big map and it is easy to see where your home is and which route to take to get to the destination. Please use the index at the back. For example, if you have an interview, search for the street name in the index at the back of the map, then find the street on the map. The map is labeled A-W vertically and 1-32 horizontally. For example, the index indicates that Dunn Avenue is at S-T 14. So, find the letters S and T on the map vertically and 14 horizontally. Dunn Avenue will be located on the map where they intersect. The MapArt street guide too has an index at the back.

If you buy a GPS (Global Positioning System), it will be quite easy to travel by vehicle or public transport. My GPS is a Garmin Nuvi 255 and it is pretty good. It shows the directions and also has a voice that guides you (for example, it says, "Turn right in five hundred feet").

Another good way to find a location is to just enter the postal code of the address and search in Google. A map with the location highlighted will appear.

Google maps at http://maps.google.ca are also good. Here, once you've found a location, you can also get driving directions and distance by clicking the "Get Directions" link. When you zoom in (by clicking the "+" sign) to the closest view, you can see the actual address in a picture format. For example, if it is a house, you can see the actual house.

If you need a taxi, just dial #TAXI and you will be connected to a taxi. If your vehicle needs a battery boost to start and there is no one around to help you, do the same and ask a taxi driver to give you a boost. They usually charge $20.

> Me: Yes ! Remember? Teacher said we would have a test today, rain or shine?
> Friend: Man, are you OK? What's good about that?
> Me: It's snowing !

If you would like to travel to the Niagara Falls casino, take a Safeway Tours bus. Visit www.Safewaytours.net for the schedule.

The good thing is that the casino is right in front of the falls so you can visit the casino and the falls at the same time. The first round trip is $25 and thereafter it is just $5, but for this special price, you need to obtain the Players Card and use it at the casino every time you take the bus. If you didn't use it the previous trip, you might have to pay $25 instead of $5. I've taken the bus few times and thoroughly enjoyed it. They usually play a movie during the daytime. At night, they usually don't because some people prefer to sleep.

I must really stress that I don't want you to get addicted to gambling but I mention this deal only because you also get to view the falls for a good price. It is very important to know your limits when gambling at any casino. I've seen people getting addicted and losing thousands of dollars and seriously damaging their future. Drinking while gambling is bad, and don't try to think to recover the money lost by gambling more. If you think that you or someone you know is addicted to gambling, please contact the Centre for Addiction and Mental Health (CAMH).

Website :
www.camh.net

Mailing address:
Problem Gambling Institute of Ontario

33 Russell Street
Toronto, Ontario
M5S 2S1

For help or information about treatment:
Call (416) 535-8501, ext. 3912; ask for the Intake Coordinator

Fax: 416 599-1324
E-mail: gambling@camh.net

If you are travelling outside of Toronto by air, try a "Flight Centre" location. They do have some good deals and at the time of writing, they will match a competitor's offer if flights are available and give a $20 coupon that can be used towards the purchase of another ticket. As these offers could change, please contact them directly to see if they still apply. You can also try Porter Airlines at www.flyporter.com or 1-888-619-8622.

If you want to see how the traffic is on the highways, you can listen to 680 news, which is at 680 AM frequency on the radio. They have traffic and weather reports at :01, :11, :21, :31, :41 and :51 past the hour, with five-day forecasts of weather at :21 and :51 past the hour. I have set my AM radio station to 680 so after listening to music on my favorite FM channel, as soon as I switch my radio to AM at the correct time, I have the traffic update. If you like to see the highways visually, go to www.680news.com, click the traffic tab, and click any of the dark blue dots on the map to see the view of the camera at that location.

The website for GO transit (Go trains and buses) is www.gotransit.com and their phone number is 1-888-438-6646. You can use these buses and trains to go to areas not covered by the city transit systems (TTC, Brampton Transit) of the GTA. Some prefer to use GO transit even if their route is covered by a transit system of GTA because it could be faster and more comfortable because there are fewer stops. The Greyhound bus terminal website is www.greyhound.ca and their phone number is 1-800-661-8747. You can use their buses for long distance trips such as to USA. You may also try a train of Via Rail by visiting www.viarail.ca or contacting them at 1-888-842-7245. This would be more comfortable for long distance trips since you can walk around in the train and there are more facilities.

Chapter 8—Buying a Car

Get a driver's license

Ontario has a Graduated Licensing System (GLS) that takes at least twenty months to complete, so the sooner you start it, the better. If you have driving experience and a driving license from another country, the process might be quicker, so please contact the Ministry of Transportation for more information. If you have a driver's license, you might be able to find an easier or better job. For example, if it's hard for you to do a factory job and you prefer a security job, having a driver's license greatly improves your chances. The driver's license can also be used as an ID. Also, even if you have the money to buy a vehicle, especially for the winter, without a license, you won't be able to drive it.

In summary, here are the steps:

1. Get the G1 license by passing the vision test and written test on the rules of the road and traffic signs.

2. After holding the G1 licence for a minimum of twelve months (only eight months if you successfully complete a Ministry-approved Beginner Driver Education Course), pass the G1 road test to get the G2 license.

3. After holding the G2 licence for a minimum of twelve months, pass the G2 road test to get the G license.

As these steps could change, please visit the Ministry of Transportation website for up-to-date information. At some of the levels above, there are conditions with which you have to drive. To see the full details, please visit:

www.mto.gov.on.ca/english/dandv/driver/gradu/index.shtml.

The number for driver and vehicle licensing is (416) 235-2999 or 1-800-387-3445

The Ministry of Transportation's website is www.mto.gov.on.ca.

Change your address for driving license within six days of a move

You have to change your driving license address within six days of moving by using the ServiceOntario online change of address service or taking the change of information form that comes with your licence to a ServiceOntario Kiosk or a Driver and Vehicle Licence Issuing Office. You can also or mail it, or a signed letter, stating your driver's license number, your old and new addresses to:

ServiceOntario

P.O. Box 9200
Kingston, ON K7L 5K4

As procedures could change, please visit the Ministry of Transportation website to confirm this procedure before following it.

Have to change parking ticket address separately

When you move, if you have disputed a parking ticket in the past and decided to challenge it in court, please remember to change your address at the Ontario Parking Authority by calling (416) 665-5672. When you change your address for the driving license, your address at the Ontario Parking Authority does not change automatically so you have to call them separately to change it. If not, the notice to appear in court will go to the old address and if you don't get it and don't appear in court, you will be guilty of the offense.

Great twenty-four hour garages (for vehicle repairs)

Just one month ago I found an amazing garage for vehicle repairs. It's Bento's Auto and Tire Centre Limited at 2000 Dundas Street West, (416) 588-4444 or (416) 533-2500. Please keep this address and phone numbers in your wallet because they are open twenty-four hours a day and all seven days of the week. In case you do not have their address or phone number with you, just remember that it's on the right side a bit north after the first traffic lights where College Street West and Dundas Street West meet. The address is easy to remember too (2000 Dundas Street West). Their prices and service are good and they were also named the "2009 Garage of the Year" by the SSGM (Service Station and Garage Management) magazine. Here's a true story. On a Sunday night when I was parked on a street at around 9:30 p.m., I found out that I had a flat tire. Talk about bad timing. It was my spare tire too and all of the garages I knew at that time were closed. Parking on that street after midnight is not allowed. I was considering several options and thought I need to calm down so I went to the nearby Coffee Time to buy a coffee and a muffin. When I asked, the person working there did not know a garage open at that time but the customer he was serving told me about Bento's Auto and that it is open 24 hrs. Boy, was I glad or what! A friend gave me and my flat tire a ride to Bento's Auto and they not only fixed my tire but also drove me to the location and replaced the tire for me (after I asked for some help and told them that I had never changed a tire in my life). Talk about service! I tried another twenty-four hour garage once called King Automotive, at King and Strachan, to fix a tire and was happy with their service. Their phone number is (416) 760-8100 and address is 111 Strachan Ave. Unit 3, Toronto, ON M6J 2S7. If you are way too far from Bento Auto, just ask a taxi driver where you can find a twenty-hour garage. They might know because some of them work overnight and might need repairs in the middle of the night. That's how I found King Automotive above.

Get the CAA Membership

Please get the CAA (Canadian Automobile Association) membership once you buy a car.

Here are just some of the benefits:

1. 24/7 roadside assistance.

   They will help you when you:

   - run out of gas

   - have a flat tire

   - are locked out of your car

   - have a problem starting the vehicle.

2. Discounts and savings opportunities

   You can get discounts for various products and services offered by different companies by presenting your CAA membership card.

3. Competitive insurance rates

4. Expert automotive advice

At the time of writing, the CAA Basic membership is $64 and the CAA plus membership is $101 plus taxes. For more information and see the up to date prices, call 1-800-564-6222 or go to www.caasco.com/membership-savings/member-benefits/.

It is very important to keep an extra key in your pocket in case you lock the doors with the key inside. Just in the last twelve months I locked my key inside at least five times. It could happen to anyone, especially if you get distracted.

The website www.autotrader.ca is very popular among vehicle buyers and sellers. Their printed magazines are available for sale at gas stations, convenience stores, magazine stands, and other places. You can also search for vehicles online at the website above. I was having a hard time selling my old car years ago but sold it within a week after placing an ad in this magazine. Some were even willing to pay a higher price than I advertised!

Buying a new car

Here are some things to consider:

* How much can you afford?

* What are the safety ratings?

* What is the fuel efficiency, i.e., kilometers per liter?

* How much will insurance cost?

* Is there enough space for you and your family?

* What is the resale value?

* What are the potential repairs and maintenance costs in the future?

* What is the best color for your needs? Lighter colors such as white and silver are considered safer because they can be seen better in the dark.

From what I've heard, Toyota Corolla, a midsize family sedan, is pretty good in terms of fuel efficiency, repairs, and maintenance costs.

Here are a few more tips:

- Wait for great incentives on price, financing, and warranties offered from time to time.

- Get your credit report and credit score from www.equifax.ca or www.transunion.ca. When you know your credit score, the salesperson cannot tell you that they'll have to charge you a higher price or higher interest rate for financing by claiming you have bad credit.

- Consider the pros and cons of financing and leasing. For example, if you finance, your monthly payments will be higher but at the end, you will own the vehicle. There might be tax advantages if you have a business and lease a vehicle.

> Me: Oh, doctor, please help me. Every night I dream that there are horrible monsters under my bed.
> Doctor: Sleep on the floor.

Buying a used car

In addition to the points mentioned in "Buying a new car" above, please also note the following:

- Get a report for the vehicle you are interested in buying from www.carfax.com. Below are some types of information that a CARFAX Report may include:

- title information, including salvaged or junked titles
- flood damage history
- total loss accident history
- odometer readings
- number of owners

- accident indicators, such as airbag deployments
- state emissions inspection results
- service records
- vehicle use (taxi, rental, lease, etc.)
- If buying from a dealer, ask if there are any other fees (administration fees, etc.). To see if a dealer is an authorized one, go to the Ontario Motor Vehicle Industry Council's website at https://ewconsumers.omvic.on.ca/Search/Dealer.aspx and search for the dealer under the business name to see if their Status appears as "Registered".
- Ask if the car is Certified and Emissions tested.
- Test it on the highway as well as on city streets.
- After you have checked it but before buying, show it to a mechanic. If the dealer refuses to let you take the vehicle, you can bring a mechanic from a nearby garage after you've checked and selected one vehicle.

Chapter 9—Handling the Winter

Learning to dress properly for the winter is very important. If you don't, not only will you feel uncomfortable, you could also worsen sicknesses, such as asthma, that you might already have.

A good starting point is to look at the CP24 news channel on TV. It will show the temperature expected in the morning, afternoon, evening, and night. It also shows the expected weather for the week and other weather indicators such as wind speed, humidity, rain, wind chill, and sunshine.

> A man falls from his twentieth story apartment balcony. While falling, he sees his wife in the kitchen preparing dinner. So he shouts, "Honey, don't cook for me …"

In the winter I always look at the wind speed in addition

to the temperature. When it is windy, it feels much colder because the cold air is pushed inside your clothes through openings in the areas such as face, ankles, and wrists. If the wind speed is high, dress as you would if the temperature itself was colder.

Wind chill is the felt air temperature on exposed skin due to wind. The wind chill temperature is always lower than the air temperature. Take the wind chill into account when dressing in the winter.

Because of the sun, daytime (especially afternoon) is usually warmer than night time. If you need to do something outside, try to schedule it in the daytime.

Layering

Layering is very important to keep warm in the winter. To learn about layering, please go to the Mountain Equipment Co-op website as shown below. It's just around one page long but the information is very valuable.

1. Go to www.mec.ca.
2. Click the "Learn" tab at the top.
3. Click "Clothing" at the top right corner.
4. Click "Dressing for the Outdoors" in the middle left.
5. Click "Layering your clothing" in the middle left.

Wear at least two layers in the winter. The outer layer is your winter jacket. If you think it is a hassle to remove the inner layer, at least use a jacket with a full length zipper as the inner layer. This way, you will be able to remove it easily. There will be some heat loss because of the zipper, but it's better than having no inner layer at all.

Chapter 10—Saving

Your main goal is to save a minimum of $800 per month with low risk, which means $50,967.70 in five years at 3 percent interest per year. Time flies, and if you don't do this, after 5 years you will wish you had. Please note that you will probably have to reduce this dollar target if you plan to sacrifice time for studying, volunteering, etc.

As you save money like this, please invest it wisely as explained in Chapter 11, "Investing." Some might argue that $50,967.70 is not much. But please remember that, if you do not have a firm and simple goal like this, you might tend to overspend, borrow from credit cards, etc., and after five years, you'll find yourself with some loans and credit cards and little or no assets. So, in that light, having $50,000 after five years is good because you will have learned how to save and will continue to do so. You will also be able to invest that $50,000 in a house and/or a business to generate even more savings.

But, please be careful when investing and consider an investment with low risk.

Another way to look at this $50,000, especially if you migrated to Canada from a developing country, is to see how much it is worth in the country from which you migrated. This way, you can at least be happy that you achieved something while establishing yourself in Canada and experiencing some of the good aspects of Canada.

In the remainder of this chapter, I will give you some ideas to help you to save the minimum $800 per month.

If you live alone, consider sharing an apartment or house with few of your friends. This way, you can share costs such as rent, Hydro, TV, Internet, computer, etc. If planned properly, you can also have a great time. For example, a few years ago, I shared an apartment with two more friends and had a great time while saving money. It was so much fun that another friend even said that he didn't mind even sleeping on the sofa if he could join us.

You could also save time on cooking, cleaning, grocery shopping, etc., by setting up a schedule and splitting up the work amongst yourselves.

Each person would cook two days of the week (totaling six days) and one day of the week we would buy some food from a Sri Lankan restaurant for a change. One person would be responsible for cleaning one week and the next week another. Almost every weekend, we would have a small party or get together at our place or a friend's place, and in the summer we would go to a beach or a special event like a musical show, CNE (Canadian National Exhibition), etc. Good times for sure.

If you want to travel by car to work, consider carpooling with some friends that work in the same area where you do.

> *Doctor: I have some good news and some bad news.*
> *Patient: What's the good news?*
> *Doctor: You have twenty-four hours to live.*
> *Patient: What! If that's the good news, then what's the bad news?*
> *Doctor: I forgot to call you yesterday.*

Goodwill has 50 percent off (except brand new goods and auction items) sales on some Fridays. Goodwill is a store where you can buy used items donated by others. So, visit www.goodwill.on.ca and ask them when the next 50 percent off sale is going to be. This is especially good for furniture items.

Try these sites for coupons and flyers:

www.redflagdeals.com

www.flyerland.ca

www.smartcanucks.ca

Try to buy groceries in bulk or in bigger sizes to get discounts. And if you see items such as soap, toilet paper, etc., on sale, try to stock up. When buying a more expensive item like a TV, if you and few of your friends would like to buy the same product, go to few shops together and ask for a discount since a few of you will be buying.

Hirantha Nandasena

The three e's (efficient, effective and economical)

I would urge you to be efficient, effective, and economical. In management science, these are known as the 3 E's and are considered important for the success of a business. Especially since you are new to Toronto and Canada, these 3 E's are important for your success too. At the beginning, you need time to learn various things and it might take you longer to get things done since the environment and the way things are done are new. By learning different ways to be efficient, you'll free up valuable time that you could use for all of these activities. Here are just some examples that will save you time.

Use a Bluetooth device or earphone to talk on your cell phone. This way you can save some time by making necessary calls while you are doing something else like grocery shopping, walking, or commuting. But please do not do this when you are driving.

If possible, do things during non-busy times. If possible, do grocery shopping weekday mornings when other people are at work.

> *I still don't know why I once got fired on the first day of a new job even after I worked till late evening on the computer.*
>
> *My boss was happy at first and asked what I did till the evening. I told him that I noticed that the keyboard alphabets were not in order, so I fixed it.*

If you need to go somewhere far, try to do that during a time that you think the roads will not be busy, such as Sunday or weekday late mornings. You could also check 680news for the traffic update or check the highway cameras on their website. I had to go to Oakville today from my home at Keele and 401 and I saved an hour and a half by doing this.

Keep a list of grocery items you need to buy and buy them once a month for the whole month. This way you save time and money. Some items, like bread and milk, will have to be bought weekly, but it saves time and money to buy the majority once a month.

Select a cell phone plan where you have enough daytime minutes for yourself. This way, you can control your cell phone bill and make it cheaper. I know some people who end up paying cell phone bills amounting to more than $100 dollars each month. Having more daytime minutes also gives you more flexibility and makes life easier; you won't have to wait till the evening to return every call. If you are free earlier, you can return the call right away without having to go searching for a land phone. For example, at the time of writing, Fido has a $40 per month plan for two thousand anytime minutes. There are other charges like system access fee, 911 fee, etc., so please visit their website for more details.

Rain Checks

OK, let's talk about shopping. If you see something very interesting at a discount in a store flyer online or at home (in flyers delivered by mail), try calling the nearest branches of that store to see if they have the item in stock. Usually, items advertised in a flyer at a bargain price sell out pretty quickly. If the flyer does not say "No rain checks" for that item, you can go to the store and get a rain check. A rain check means you are reserving the item at the advertised discount price to purchase when it is re-stocked in the store.

Good products

Here are just few popular products that I have found to perform quite well.

Oxyclean or Tide to Go instant stain removers are pretty good to remove stains from clothes etc. Easy Off oven cleaner is good to clean the grease of ovens. Fantastic spray is very good for general cleaning. If some areas are hard to clean, spray this and leave it for few minutes before wiping the dirt off.

Good Stores

Here are just some of the stores I've found where you can get some good deals. If you need cell phone accessories such as a charger, car charger, etc., try Mobilink at the Dufferin Mall. The prices are good and it's very close to the entrance facing the traffic lights. You don't have to walk all over the mall to find it. Try XScargo for household items such as small appliances (rice cookers, kitchen scales, etc.), furniture, etc. I've found their prices to be pretty low. For example, at the time of writing, they are selling a small computer desk for just $19.99 and just one month ago I bought a small rice cooker for just $9.83. For more details, please visit www.XScargo.com. No Frills and Metro are good for grocery shopping. Items at No Frills tend to be cheaper but Metro is open twenty-four hours. For regular shopping (clothes, shoes, stationery, cleaning supplies, electronics, etc), try Wal-Mart. Their prices are pretty low and they are quite popular among Canadians. I've mentioned these stores for the beginning, when you first arrive here. Later on, please ask your friends and colleagues where you can find some great deals.

If you want to make sure that the store closest to you has the service (e.g., auto repair, pharmacy etc.) you are looking for, select the service you want when you are searching for the closest store on their website.

Twenty-four hour restaurants

Here are just two twenty-four hour restaurants in case you need a bite in the middle of the night:

Vesta Lunch
at Bathurst and Dupont
474 Dupont St.
Toronto, ON M5R 1W6
Tel: (416) 537-4318

Hirantha Nandasena

The Lakeview Restaurant
At Dundas and Ossington
1132 Dundas St. W.
Toronto, ON M6J 1X2
Tel: (416) 850-8886
Email: <u>handshakes@thelakeviewrestaurant.ca</u>
<u>www.thelakeviewrestaurant.ca</u>

There are also some other restaurants open late. I like Hong Shing (chili chicken on rice is awesome) at University and Dundas, which is downtown. They are open till 4:30 a.m. but, just like the other restaurants, please call before you go there to make sure. It's quite popular among club goers because it's not far from the clubs.

Tel: (416) 977-3338

195 Dundas St. West

Toronto,ON.M5G 1C7

There are also some restaurants open late on Spadina Road near College Street. Quite a few Tim Hortons stores are open twenty-four hours. You should be able to find a twenty-four hour store by going to their website.

Creating a credit history

Creating a credit history is very important in Canada. You'll need a good credit rating to secure a mortgage for a house, take a vehicle loan, get a credit card, etc. To create a good credit history, obtain a secured credit card and/or a department store credit card. A secured credit card is a credit card that the bank will give you if you have placed a deposit with them as a security. It is easier to obtain a credit card from a department store than a bank so try HBC (Hudson's Bay Company, i.e. The Bay), Sears, Canadian Tire, Wal-Mart, etc. Don't take too many credit cards because it could damage your credit rating. If you pay off your balance every month, you'll have a better credit rating. If you don't pay at least your minimum monthly payment, your credit rating will get worse.

If you want to buy something, pay with your credit card and settle it at the end of the month. One important factor that affects your credit rating is how much of your available credit you have used up. For example, if your credit limit is $5,000 and you have used up $4,900 of it and don't pay it off at the end of the month, it's not that good. Another factor that will affect your credit rating is if you have been paying at least your minimum payment on time.

Although it is important to create a credit history, many people get into trouble by signing up for and using the full amount of quite a few credit cards. When they do that, they get stuck in a never ending cycle where they struggle to pay the minimum monthly payments from their pay checks. So, please be very careful. If you get into this position, it would be very hard to save $50,000 in five years as mentioned in Chapter 10, "Saving."

After a year or two, you can obtain your credit report and credit score by visiting www.transunion.ca or www.equifax.ca.

How to get rid of your change

If you have too much change in your pockets, always try to use it up when you are shopping. When I am in a line at a coffee shop, I pull out my change so I won't waste mine and others' time when I am paying. If I still have lots of change, I just dump it into a coin bag I have at home. When the bag is getting full, I take it to a Metro grocery store and use their Coinstar (coin changing) machine to convert the coins into bills. Please note that there is a 11.9 percent fee, meaning, for every $10 bill you get, you'll have to pay $1.19. I know it's not cheap but it's an option if you don't like dealing with small change.

Be careful when lending money

Friend, please do not lend money to people you've known for just few months. I say this because people might try to take advantage of you if they know you are a new immigrant. Usually, these people are smooth talkers who will come up with a sad and urgent story to make you feel like you have to help them out. Please refer them to a government institution or their close friends or relatives for help. Or try to help them to get a part time job to earn some extra cash.

Emergency fund

Please keep an emergency fund in a bank account. While I hope you do not, you could be faced with situations like job loss, accident, sudden need to travel overseas, health issues, etc. Because many people have their own problems, they might not be able to help you. Having said that, please remember that you can seek government assistance if the need arises.

Make your own coffee

You could save a lot by doing this. For example, if you buy

three coffees a day, you would be spending around $120 ($1.33 X 3 X 30) dollars a month. Instead, with just around $20 or less per month, you can make your own coffee at home. I like my one-cup Black & Decker Brew 'N Go coffee maker. I buy two or three Tim Horton's coffee powder (Fine Grind) tins of 369g a month and the coffee is ready in four minutes. Because it has a permanent filter, I don't even have to change filters and it is very easy to wash.

A cheap way to go to the airport

Instead of spending $15 to 50 or more for a taxi, you can save a lot by taking a TTC bus for a one-way fare (currently $3) from the Kipling, Lawrence West subway stations or other locations. For a list of all of the locations, please go to:

www3.ttc.ca/Riding_the_TTC/Airport_service.jsp

How to get out of a cell phone contract

If you signed up for a contract (typically two or three years) for a cell phone and you want to cancel it, you will have to pay a big cancellation fee. This could be even $200 or more depending on how many months are left in your contract. Instead, go to http://www.cellswapper.com/ or http://www.cellplandepot.com/ and place an ad to find someone who is willing to take over the rest of your contract.

Chapter 11—Investing

As a general principle, do not put all of your eggs in one basket. If you do that and lose or damage that basket, you lose all of your eggs. Do not invest all of your money in one thing. Try to invest in few things such as savings accounts, RRSPs, stocks, house, business, etc. Also, if possible, try to look for investments with a minimum return. For example, there are some RRSPs that guarantee you a minimum return.

Registered Retirement Savings Plan

An RRSP is a good way to save for your retirement. You can also withdraw up to $25,000 from your RRSP under the HBP (Home Buyers Plan) to buy or build a home for yourself as a first-time home buyer. You are not considered a first-time home buyer if you or your spouse or common-law partner owned a home that you occupied as your principle place of residence during the period beginning January 1 of the fourth year before the year of withdrawal and ending thirty-one days before your withdrawal. For example, if someone sold their home in 2008, he/she can participate in the HBP only in 2013 or after. The amount you borrow has to be paid back within fifteen years. To see all of the conditions that need to be satisfied, please visit the Canada Revenue Agency's (CRA) website at www.cra-arc.gc.ca/menu-eng.html and do a search for "Home Buyers Plan."

There is a tax benefit for contributing to an RRSP as you can reduce your taxable income and any income you earn in the RRSP is usually exempt from tax for the time the funds remain in the plan. However, you generally have to pay tax when you cash in, make withdrawals, or receive payments from the plan.

Registered Education Savings Plan

Here is a description of RESPs (Registered Education Savings Plan) from the Canada Revenue Agency's website:

"With the help of an RESP you, as a parent, friend, or family member, can start putting aside money for a child's post-secondary education. Your contributions can grow surprisingly quickly when you use this special savings account, as the Government of Canada offers the Canada Education Savings Grant and the Canada Learning Bond exclusively to RESP subscribers …

… upon enrolling in a qualifying educational program—a course of study that lasts at least three consecutive weeks, with a minimum of ten hours of instruction or work per week— the child named in your plan will become eligible to receive payments from the RESP to help cover the costs of education after high school."

For all of the conditions and more details, please visit the CRA website and do a search for RESP.

> Teacher: Did you father help your with your homework?
> Me: No, he did it all by himself.

Another investment that you might want to consider is a part-time business. Please note that this could be a risky investment. If you want to reduce your risk, you could consider purchasing a franchise (perhaps home-based to save rent) with a proven track record, i.e., one where franchisees have recovered their investment fairly quickly and the failure rate is low.

A very popular book on saving and investing that I can recommend is *"The Wealthy Barber"*, by David Chilton. *"Stop working. Here's how you can"*, by Derek Foster, is also pretty good and is available for purchase at the website for my book at www.successintoronto.com/other-useful-books.

Chapter 12—Cooking in Less than Twenty Minutes

Cooking your own food at home rather than eating from outside is great because it is cheaper and healthier. I say healthier because you know you won't put MSG in your recipes and you can ensure the food and utensils are properly washed.

It may seem like you'll never be able to learn to cook tasty dishes but the following tips will help you. Trust me, I used to think like that, but after lots of practice now I can cook some tasty dishes and have learned a bit of the art of cooking.

> *Child 1: Oh my god, my dad is so afraid of thunder that he sleeps under the bed.*
>
> *Child 2: That's nothing, my dad is so afraid of the dark that he sleeps with our neighbor lady when my mom's away.*

Try searching on YouTube to learn how to cook your favorite dish. The good thing with this is that you can actually see how it is being cooked and it is much better than reading a book. I've seen some good videos that are only five to ten minutes long. Like I said in an earlier chapter, some cultural sites have recipes and perhaps videos too. Buy a rice cooker if you like rice.

At least when I was new to cooking—and sometimes even now—to ensure I cook properly, while watching an expert cook I write down the exact measurements (eg: number of teaspoons, cups etc) and timings and then try to prepare the dish with the same taste by following those exact measurements and timings.

Here are some items that are easy to prepare within twenty minutes or less:

- Salmon
- Eggs
- Sausages
- Beans

- Salad
- Sandwiches
- Instant noodles
- Rice
- Dhal

I've found that the Ligo brand of salmon is good because the pieces are bigger and they don't break apart much when you cook them. I like the ones with tomato paste.

If you are into Indian food and want to cook something tasty with less effort, try the "Kitchens of India" pastes, such as chicken curry paste, vegetable biryani paste, etc. I used to just cut some boneless chicken breasts, put few cups of water and a packet of chicken curry paste, and let it cook into a delicious dish even without adding anything else like onions, tomatoes, or other spices. Ask your friends who share similar tastes what products are good for cooking.

Chapter 13—A Quick and Easy Way to Improve English

> *Friend: Man, I found this great pickup line.*
> *Me: Really? Let me hear it.*
> *Friend: "Come with me if you want to live."*

Here's what I did when I was sixteen to dramatically improve my communication in English. I don't know if there is some kind of system like this or if people just call it a vocabulary. I went through an entire dictionary and picked the words I thought I might have to use on a weekly basis. Then, I would read this list once a day or at least once a week. It takes only five to ten minutes to read. If I had exams, interviews, etc., I would read the list daily and right before the exam or interview. Because I read it daily, those words were in my memory (at least vaguely) so when I was trying to search for the right word when speaking or writing, it would come up much more quickly. I also became better at spelling words.

Hirantha Nandasena

If you are not sure if you can learn English properly, think of it this way: If a baby born in Canada can learn English within two to three years, so can you. Just let go of this doubt and practice by reading and speaking often. Practice makes perfect. Below is my full list. If you think you won't need all of these words, you could highlight the words that you think you would use with a highlighter pen and add to the end of the list any other words that you think you'll need.

Absentminded	Assemble
Absolute	Assign
Absorb	Assist
Abstract	Associate
Accumulate	Assume
Accuse	Assure
Accustom	Asterisk
Acknowledge	Atmosphere
Admire	Attach
Adopt	Attain
Adore	Attempt
Adverse	Attitude
Affection	Await
Ahead	Aware
Allocate	Awkward
Alternative	Barrier
Analyse, analyze	Base
Anticipate	On behalf of
Anxious	Beneath
Apparent	Benefit
Appear	Besides
Appreciate	Beware

Approve
Argue
Arise
Brilliant
Burden
Capable
Capacity
Capture
Casual
Category
Cater
Cease
Ceremonious
Claim
Clarify
Comprehensive
Compromise
Concept
Concern
Concise
Conclude
Confess
Configuration
Conflict
Confront
Conquer
Conscious
Consecutive
Consequences
Consist
Consolidate

Beyond
Bias
Branch
Cope
Corruption
Crucial
Cue
Decline
Decompose
Decrement
Dedicate
Deliberate
Delicate
Delight
Demand
Desperate
Determine
Devote
Differ
Differentiate
Disaster
Disguise
Distinguish
Duplicate
Duration
Efficient
Eliminate
Emphasis
Enhance
Enormous
Ensure

Constitute
Consume
Contradict
Convenient
Convince
Exhaust
Expand
Expose
Extreme
As a matter of fact
Familiar
Fantastic
Fault
Favor
Feature
Focus
Frequent
Frustrate
Fundamental
Generous
Gradually
Grasp
Grateful
Grievance
Horrible
Illegal
Implement
Inconvenience
Indent
Independent
Indicate

Entire
Especial
Establish
Estimate
Exaggerate
Interchange
Interpret
Intrude
Invaluable
Irritate
Issue
Legal
Lenient
Local
Magnificent
Manage
Minor
Miracle
Misplace
Moderate
Modest
Monotonous
Narrow
Neglect
Negotiate
Neither
Nonsense
Obedient
Observe
Obstacle
Obtain

Individual	Obvious
Influence	Occasion
Insist	Occupy
For instance	Occur
Instant	Odd
Insufficient	Opponent
Intend	Outstanding
Overdo	Resolve
Overflow	Reveal
Overjoyed	Reverse
Panic	Revolution
Particular	Routine
Penetrate	Ruin
Perfect	Sarcastic
Permit	Scatter
Pioneer	Scramble
Polite	Scratch
Predict	Sequence
Prefer	Session
Profession	Severe
Profile	Shatter
Programme	Simultaneous
Progress	Skid
Prohibit	Slide
Promote	Slip
Property	Slogan
Proportional	Snare
Propose	Spare
Quarrel	Specific
Queue	Splendid
Raise	Spit

Reassure	Starve
Reconstitute	Statue
Recruit	Steady
Regain	Steer
Regular	Stingy
Relief	Stink
Reluctant	Strategy
Remote	Structure
Reputation	Subconscious
Subordinate	Unlike
Superb	Unnecessary
Superior	Unreasonable
Superstition	Unsuccessful
Surface	Urban
Surplus	Verify
Swap, swop	Violent
Syllabus	Voluntary
Sympathy	Weird
Symptom	Whisper
Tabular	Isolate
Tangible	Community
Tempt	Component
Tension	Gradually
Terrific	Grasp
Territory	Prefer
Thorough	Territory
Thrash	Predict
Tragedy	Comment
Transaction	Tempt
Transform	Colleague
Transparent	Precise

Tremendous	Praise
Ultimate	Collapse
Unavoidable	Posses
Uncommon	Portable
Unconscious	Fragile
Underestimate	Clash
Underneath	
Undertake	
Unexpected	
Unfortunate	
Unique	

The Government of Canada, in cooperation with provincial governments, school boards, community colleges, and immigrant and community organizations, offers free language training across the country. This program is called LINC (Language Instruction for Newcomers to Canada). To find out where you can take LINC classes in your area, go to the Services for Newcomers page of the CIC website at www.servicesfornewcomers.cic.gc.ca.

I've left the rest of this page and next page blank so you can add more words to the list above if needed.

Chapter 14—Assistance

Settlement assistance (overall)

Please visit each of the websites below for at least ten minutes each for more information about the services offered by these organizations. They can help you to settle here in many ways (jobs, housing, training, directions, and much more).

The Host Program
www.servicecanada.gc.ca/eng/goc/host.shtml

Newcomers
www.citizenship.gov.on.ca/english/newcomers.shtml

Newcomer Settlement Program
www.citizenship.gov.on.ca/english/keyinitiatives/newcomer.shtml

Newcomer settlement agencies by location
www.citizenship.gov.on.ca/english/newcomers/agencies.shtml

Global experience Ontario
www.ontarioimmigration.ca/en/geo/index.htm

211 Toronto (a directory of community, social, health and government services)
www.211toronto.ca/index.jsp
settlement.org
www.settlement.org/index.asp

City of Toronto Immigration
www.toronto.ca/immigration

Ontario Immigration
www.ontarioimmigration.ca

Legal aid

If you need a lawyer but cannot afford it and have low or no income, contact Legal Aid Ontario. They give low-income people access to a range of legal services and they help almost four thousand people every day.

You'll have to meet their strict financial eligibility limits. You might be asked to contribute toward the cost of their legal fees.

Here are their contact details:

Tel: 1-800-668-8258
Fax: (416) 979-8669
TTY: 1-866-641-8867
www.legalaid.on.ca

Employment Insurance (EI)

Employment Insurance (EI) provides regular benefits to

individuals who lose their jobs through no fault of their own and are available for and able to work, but can't find a job. If you voluntarily quit your job without just cause or if you are fired due to your own misconduct, you might not be paid regular benefits.

To be eligible for regular benefits you must show that in the last fifty-two weeks or since your last claim (the qualifying period), you have worked for the required number of insurable hours. Most people will need between four hundred twenty and seven hundred insurable hours of work in their qualifying period to qualify, depending on the unemployment rate in their region at the time of filing their claim for benefits.

A minimum of nine hundred ten hours in the qualifying period may be needed to qualify, for example, if you are in the work force for the first time or if you are re-entering the work force after an absence of two years.

To find out if you can receive EI benefits, you must submit an application for EI online or in person at your Service Canada Centre. You will need the ROE (Record of Employment) issued by your employer.

The basic benefit rate is 55 percent of your average insured earnings up to a yearly maximum insurable amount of $43,200 (i.e., a maximum payment of $457 per week).

You could receive a higher benefit rate if you are in a low-income family (i.e., net income less than or equal to $25,921 per year) with children and you or your spouse receive the Canada Child Tax Benefit (CCTB). You are then entitled to the Family Supplement.

Regular benefits can be paid from nineteen to a maximum of fifty weeks.

As the information above is likely to change, please visit the website below to view the up-to-date information.

Here are the contact details:

Tel: 1-800 206-7218.
TTY: 1-800 529-3742.
www.servicecanada.gc.ca/eng/ei/types/regular.shtml#eligible

Social Assistance

Ontario's social assistance programs help residents of Ontario who are in financial need. The programs provide:

- money to help cover the cost of basic needs for adults, such as food

- money to help cover housing costs for adults and their families, and

- employment assistance to help individuals prepare for, find and keep a job.

There are two different social assistance programs:

- Ontario Disability Support Program
- Ontario Works

For more information on the Ontario Works program, contact your nearest local Ontario Works office. For information on the Ontario Disability Support Program, contact your nearest Ontario Disability Support Program office. To locate your nearest office, try the Social Assistance Office Locator at:

www.mcss.gov.on.ca/mcss/owapp/Locator/index.aspx?lang=en

Ontario Disability Support Program

The Ontario Disability Support Program helps people with disabilities who need:

- financial help, or
- help finding a job.

If you are eligible, you may also receive health and other benefits for yourself and your family.

Ontario Works

If you need money right away to pay for food and housing, Ontario Works may be able to help you. To qualify, you must be willing to participate in activities to help you find a job. If you are eligible, you may also receive health and other benefits for yourself and your family.

To be eligible to receive help from Ontario Works, you must:

- live in Ontario
- need money right away to help pay for food and housing costs, and
- be willing to take part in activities that will help you find a job.

If you qualify, Ontario Works can provide you with:

1. Financial assistance
2. Employment assistance

1. Financial assistance

This will help you cover the costs of your basic needs (e.g., food) and housing costs, etc. The amount of money you may receive depends on your family size, income, assets and housing costs. Use the Eligibility Estimator at the following website address to find out if you may qualify for Ontario Works benefits:

www.mcss.gov.on.ca/mcss/owapp/Estimator/Preamble.aspx?lang=en

Depending on your outcome, you may be required to contact your local Ontario Works office either by phone or in person. Ontario Works staff will talk with you about your situation and you can decide if you want to complete an application.

If you qualify for Ontario Works, you may also be eligible to receive a variety of other benefits such as:

- prescription drug and dental coverage
- eyeglasses
- diabetic supplies
- moving or eviction costs
- employment-related costs
- employment assistance to help you prepare for and find a job.

2. Employment assistance

Ontario Works can give you practical help to prepare for and find a job by:

- working with you to determine what you need to become employed, and
- helping you develop a plan based on your skills, experience and circumstances.

Some examples of the services provided are, workshops, referrals to job counseling or training programs, information on who's hiring, access to basic education, access to telephones, faxes, computers, and job banks.

As the information above is likely to change, please contact a Social Assistance Office to obtain the up-to-date information.

OSAP (Ontario Student Assistance Program)

OSAP provides eligible Ontario students with financial aid to help pay for education-related costs such as tuition, books, living costs, and transportation. Grants, bursaries, scholarships, fellowships, debt reduction, interest relief, work study, or loans are the types of aid provided.

The Ontario portion of all OSAP loans is interest free and payment free for the first six months after you graduate. You can also earn up to $103 per week during your studies without affecting your OSAP payments.

If OSAP does not fully meet your education costs, you may be eligible to receive aid from your institution through the Ontario's Student Access Guarantee.

Here are the contact details:
Tel: 1-877-672-7411
TTY: 1-800-465-3958
https://osap.gov.on.ca/OSAPPortal

As the information above could change, please visit their website to view the up-to-date information.

Silverman Helps

If you think that you have been treated unfairly by an organization, you may contact Peter Silverman at the CFRB radio station. He hosts "The Peter Silverman Show" where he tries to resolve such issues. It's on Saturday mornings from 11 a.m. to noon on NEWSTALK 1010. His e-mail address is silverman@cfrb.com. The CFRB is an AM radio station broadcasted on 1010kHz. I've been treated unfairly in the past and even before contacting Mr. Silverman, just the mention of his name to the other party usually resolves my issue and justice is served immediately. I am truly grateful to him.

Chapter 15–Important Contact Phone Numbers and Websites

Emergency contact number

If there is an emergency (vehicle accident, robbery, etc.) dial 911 and you will be transferred to police, fire department, or ambulance service.

Telephone directory

If you don't want to go through the yellow pages or search online for a telephone number, dial 411 and mention the name of the organization, city, etc., and you will be given the phone number. Please ask your service provider how much they charge for this service. At the time of writing, Rogers Communications is charging $2.00 per call and Bell Canada is charging $2.49 per call. You will be given the number, the number will be dialed for you, and the number will be sent to your phone in a text message.

Please note that below I have given the TTY numbers too. TTY stands for "Teletypewriter." It is for the hearing impaired. Just type on the phone what you need to say, and the words will be transmitted into sound.

Here are the contact details in alphabetical order:

Canada Child Tax Benefit (CCTB)
1-800-387-1193
www.cra-arc.gc.ca/bnfts/cctb/menu-eng.html

Canada Revenue Agency
www.cra-arc.gc.ca
TTY: 1-800-665-0354

For individual income tax enquiries including personal income tax returns, installments, RRSPs, and the Working Income Tax Benefit call 1-800-959-8281.

For business and GST/HST registration, payroll, GST/HST (including rebates such as the new housing rebates), excise taxes and other levies, excise duties, corporations, sole proprietorships and partnerships, call 1-800-959-5525.

For Universal Child Care Benefit, Canada Child Tax Benefit, and related provincial and territorial programs, child disability benefit and children's special allowances, call 1-800-387-1193.

Citizenship Canada
To get information about Citizenship and Immigration (CIC) services and programs, or applications in process inside Canada, call:
1-888-242 2100
www.cic.gc.ca
TTY: 1-888-576 8502

Go Transit
For information about GO buses, trains, schedules, fares, etc.
1-888-438-6646 (GET ON GO)
TTY: 1-800-387-3652
www.gotransit.com

Greyhound Buses
1-800-661- 8747 (TRIP)
TTY: 1-800-397-7870
www.greyhound.ca

HRSDC (Human Resources and Skills Development Canada)
For information on services provided for job search, service center locations, etc.
1-800-622-6232
TTY: 1 800 926 9105
www.hrsdc.gc.ca

Legal aid
If you need a lawyer but cannot afford it and have low or no income, contact Legal Aid Ontario. They give low-income people access to a range of legal services and they help almost 4,000 people everyday. You'll have to meet their strict financial eligibility limits. You might be asked to contribute toward the cost of their legal fees. Here are their contact details:
Tel : 1-800-668-8258
Fax : 416- 979-8669
TTY : 1-866-641-8867
www.legalaid.on.ca

Ontario Ministry of Education
For information about schools, colleges, universities, etc.
1-800-387-5514
www.edu.gov.on.ca

Ontario Ministry of Health
For information on services provided, health card, etc.
www.health.gov.on.ca
Toll free: 1-866-532-3161
TTY: 1-800-387-5559
FAX: 416-314-8721
To speak to a nurse about a medical or health-related issue, call Telehealth Ontario at 1-866-797-0000. If it's a medical emergency, call 911.

Ontario Ministry of Municipal affairs and Housing
www.mah.gov.on.ca
Tel: 416-585-7041 (Customer Assistance Line)
TTY: 416-585-6991 (local call) or 1-866-220-2290 (toll free)

Ontario Ministry of Labour
For information about employment laws, your rights as an employee, health and safety at work, etc.
www.labour.gov.on.ca
Employment Standards Inquiries:
(Termination pay, unpaid wages, public holiday pay)
1-800-531-5551
TTY: 1-866-567-8893
Occupational Health and Safety Inquiries:
1-800-268-8013
Report Possible Unsafe Work Practices
1-877-202-0008
Other Inquiries:
1-866-932-7229

Ontario Ministry of Transportation
Please visit the website below for contact phone numbers as they may vary depending on the type of inquiry.
Driver and vehicle licensing:
(416) 235-2999 or 1-800-387-3445
www.mto.gov.on.ca

Ontario Wait Times
To see the wait times in Emergency Rooms or for surgery, MRIs, and CTs at hospitals in your area and across the province.
www.ontariowaittimes.ca

Passport Canada
To apply for, renew passport, etc.
1-800-567-6868
TTY: 1-866-255-7655
www.passportcanada.gc.ca

Service Ontario
For information about various services provided by the Ontario government:
www.serviceontario.ca
1-800-267-8097

For information about the SIN number:
1-800-206-7218

Taxis
Beck Taxi: (416) 751-5555
Royal Taxi: (416) 777-9222
City Taxi: (416) 740-2222
Co-op Cabs: (416) 504-2667
Crown Taxi: (416) 750-7878

Hirantha Nandasena

TTC (Toronto Transit Commission)
For information about buses, subways, streetcars, maps, fares, lost articles, etc.:
(416) 393-4636
TTY: 416-481-2523

Lost Articles:
416-393-4100
www.ttc.ca

I've left the next page blank so you can add more numbers to the list above if needed.

Chapter 16—Conclusion

Friend, I hope that I have been able to share with you some of the knowledge and experience I gained over the ten years I've been in Toronto. I would like to remind you that, as explained in Chapter 10, "Saving," your main goal is to save a minimum of $800 per month with low risk, which amounts $50,967.70 in five years at 3 percent interest per year). Time flies and if you don't do this, after five years you will wish you had. Please note that you will probably have to reduce this dollar target if you plan to sacrifice time for studying, volunteering, etc.

Please also be positive always. Reading Chapter 1, "Main Principles," and Chapter 2, "Good Things About Canada," at least once a week should help you to do so.

> *Friend 1: My dad is so fast that he gets home from work within fifteen minutes.*
> *Friend 2: That's nothing, when the boss is not around, my dad gets home from work an hour before he is supposed to finish.*

I created the website www.SuccessInToronto.com so that I can continue to help you, so please be sure to visit it from time to time. I said "from time to time" because, as time passes, I will be adding more and more useful content to the website and perhaps some deals like coupons for popular brands. It is very important to visit the website at least once after June 2011. By then I will have sold the book and got feedback and if there is something very important you should know, I'll mention it on the website and highlight it.

The more of this book that I sell, the more spare time I will have to help you and other immigrants by creating a second edition of this book (perhaps an extended version or part two) and adding valuable content to the website. Therefore, may I kindly request you to ask your friends, family, co-workers etc. to buy this book, visit the website and refer it to others (especially new immigrants). I also intend to create videos on this topic so it will be easier for you to understand. Information on how to purchase this book and the videos will be available on the website. I did not want to make this book too big with a lot of details because I know that as a new immigrant, time is very precious to you and you might not be able to spend a lot of time reading books. However, depending on the response to this book, I will most likely create an extended version of this book with more details. I would also like to get this book translated into different languages. Stay tuned for more information on the website. In conclusion, trust me when I say, "If there is a will, there is a way." You have the will, let me show you the way! All the Best !